AF540731

CORPORATE GOVERNANCE AND SUSTAINABILITY

Edited by

Dr. Suman Kalyan Chaudhury

M.Com, MBA, PGDPM & IR, LLB, Ph.D.

Reader cum Placement Officer

P.G. Department of Business Administration

Berhampur University

Berhampur

(Odisha)

DISCOVERY PUBLISHING HOUSE PVT. LTD.

NEW DELHI-110 002

Published by:
Tilak Wasan

DISCOVERY PUBLISHING HOUSE PVT. LTD.
4383/4A, Ansari Road, Darya Ganj
New Delhi-110 002 (India)
Phone : +91-11-23279245, 43596064-65
Fax : +91-11-23253475
E-mail : parul.wasan@gmail.com
discoverypublishinghouse@gmail.com
web : www.discoverypublishinggroup.com

***First Edition:* 2012**
ISBN: 978-93-5056-057-0

Corporate Governance and Sustainability

Printed at:
Shree Balaji Art Press
Delhi

Preface

In the 21st century the outlook for business appears to be a blend of high prospects for growth on the one hand and serious concerns about the impact of business on society and the environment, on the other. The extremes of all total control and freedom to business have both been found wanting by the totality of the human experiences in the 20th century and the need for a balance through harmonizing multiple stakeholders expectations is felt more and more strongly in the aftermath of series of corporate scams during the last decade in the 21st century.

Failure in corporate governance is a real threat to the future of every corporation. Corporate governance as a business ethics issue is a hundred times more powerful than the internet or globalization and can destroy your business in a week. To make matters worse, standards of corporate governance are changing rapidly in response to random events which capture public imagination. In business ethics, what was good is becoming bad and what was considered bad is now good. Standards for corporate governance that have worked for decades are looking old fashioned or immoral while other practices that raised questions are becoming totally acceptable.

Corporate governance basically denotes rule of law, transparency, accountability and protection of public interest in the management of a company's affairs in the prevailing global, competitive and digital environment. It calls for an enlightened investing community and strict regulatory regimes to protect the rights of the investors and companies to improve productivity and profitability without recourse to any means which will offend the moral, ethical and regulatory framework.

The framework for corporate governance is not only an important component affecting the long-term prosperity of companies, but it is a leading species of large genus namely, National Governance, Human Governance, Societal Governance, Economic Governance and Political Governance. Government provides necessary conditions, framework and environment to corporates to operate. There is, however, no universal recipe for good corporate governance since business environment varies from country to country. During the past 50 years industry in corporate form has moved from the periphery to the very centre of our social and economic existence. Indeed it is not inaccurate to say that we live in a corporate society. This book, written in a lucid style, aims to provide the reader with a quick overview of the subject. It explains the need for corporate governance. The book records the perceptions of different authors across the globe with the aim of giving the reader as comprehensive a picture as possible.

DR. SUMAN KALYAN CHAUDHURY

Acknowledgements

Every action requires an initiator, influencer. I am initiated into writing this book, primarily, by the inspiration provided by my students and friends in the same profession. My colleagues are always stand with for support and cheering me. Therefore, I can't but gratefully acknowledge my indebtedness to all those who have extended generous assistance in the successful accomplishment of this indispensable work. It will be a serious blunder if I forget to mention some of my colleagues— Prof. Niranjan Nayak, Center Head, Koustav Business School; Dr. Kirti Ranjan Swain, Associate Prof., IPSAR Business School, Cuttack; Dr. Ashok Kumar Panigrahi, Asst. Prof, RITEE Business School, Raipur; Prof. Ashok Kumar Panda, Dean, Astha School of Management— for their ardent encouragement and beacon guidance in bringing out this work.

I profusely thank my chairman of the institute, Er. Sundhansu Kumar Dash for his rock support and continuous push that furthered my efforts seamlessly towards quick accomplishment. My heartfelt gratitude to him.

Last but not least my heartfelt gratitude to my wife Sinu knows no bounds for her immaculate co-operation. Needless to depict, I am indebted to my family members for their love and affection and inspired me in my problem-solving while in action.

I am also much beholden to Mr. Tilak Wasan, Managing Director, Discovery Publishing House Pvt. Ltd., New Delhi for publishing the work in a record time.

DR. SUMAN KALYAN CHAUDHURY

Contents

List of Contributors

DR. KHYSER MOHD, Associate Professor and Head, Department of Business Management, Telangana University, Nizamabad, (A.P.)

TATIKONDA NEELAKANTAM, Associate Professor, Department of Business Management, S V College of Engineering and Technology, Hyderabad.

G. RADHA KRISHNA MURTHY, Assistant Professor, Department of Business Management, S V College of Engineering and Technology, Hyderabad.

K. SHYAMALA DEVI, Student, Department of Business Management, S V College of Engineering and Technology, Hyderabad.

PROF. SREEJESH. S, Assistant Professor (Marketing and Strategy) ICFAI Business School (IBS), Hyderabad, India.

DR. T. SATHYANARYANA CHARY, Head and Associate Professor, Department of Commerce, Telangana University, Dichpally, Nizamabad, A.P.

M. SWATHI, Student, Department of Business Management, S V College of Engineering and Technology, Hyderabad.

PROF. SYED JAFFER, Asst. Professor and Research Scholar, Presidency School of Management and Computer Sciences, Falaknuma, Hyderabad.

PROF. SHANTI SURESH, Associate Professor in Finance at SIES, Mumbai, Maharashtra.

Dr. Siva Kumar SNV, Professor in General Management, K J Somaiya Institute of Management Studies and Research, Mumbai, Maharashtra.

Prof. Dakshayani G.N., Assistant Professor, Government First Grade College, Bijapur, Karnataka.

Prof. Nirmala Chavan, Lecturer-in-Commerce, A.S.P. College of Commerce, Bijapur, Karnataka.

C. Chandra Shekar Reddy, Assistant Professor, Badruka College Post Graduate Center, Hyderabad, A.P.

Deo Vinayak. S., Research Scholar, Department of Commerce and Management Science Yeshwant Mahavidyalaya, Nanded, M.S.

Tammewar, Mamta S., Research Scholar Nandigram Institute of Management Studies, Nanded, M.S.

Mr. Mudholkar, G. P., Research Scholar, Nandigram Institute of Management Studies, Nanded, M.S.

Prof. Suresh Vadde, Asst. Professor, Commerce and Business Management, P.G Centre, Lal Bahadur College, S.P. Road, Warangal, A.P.

Prof. Ch. Srikanthverma, Asst. Professor, Business Management, P.G Centre, Lal Bahadur College, S.P. Road, Warangal, A.P.

F G. Jayakar Rao, Faculty of Business Management, Wesley P.G College Hydrabad, A.P.

Prof. Sanjay Kanti Das, Asstt. Professor, Commerce, Lumding College, Lumding, Nagaon, Assam.

Need of Corporate Governance in Corporate World

A model study on similarities between scams of Enron and Satyam

Dr. Khyser Mohd

ABSTRACT

Corporate governance symbolizes the value framework, the ethical framework and the moral framework under which business decisions are taken. Key elements of good corporate governance include honesty, trust and integrity, openness, performance orientation, responsibility and accountability, mutual respect, and commitment to the organization.

In the Indian context, the need for corporate governance has been highlighted because of the occurrence of scams frequently since the emergence of the concept of liberalization from 1991 such as the Harshad Mehta Scam, Ketan Parikh Scam, UTI Scam, and Bhansali Scam and so on. In the Indian corporate scene, there is a need to induct global standards to prevent scope of scams totally, if not, it can be at least reduced to the minimum. The present paper focuses on the concept of Corporate Governance with the help of two cases, viz., Enron and Satyam Computers in a comprehensive manner.

Introduction

Corporate governance represents the value framework, the ethical framework and the moral framework under which business decisions are taken. The objective of investors is to be sure that not only their capital handled effectively and adds to the creation of wealth, but also the business decisions taken in a manner which are not illegal or involving moral hazard.

Corporate governance is a multi-faceted subject. The basic theme of corporate governance is to ensure the accountability of certain individuals in an organization through mechanisms that try to reduce or eliminate the principal-agent problem. A related but separate thread of discussions focuses on the impact of a corporate governance system in economic efficiency, with a strong emphasis on shareholders' welfare. There are yet other aspects to the corporate governance subject, such as the stakeholder view and the corporate governance models around the world. Good corporate governance is characterised by a virtual commitment and adoption of ethical practices by an organisation across its entire value chain and in all of its dealings with a wide group of stakeholders.

Objective and Methodology of the Study

Corporate governance is a burning issue of the single corporate global market. It is a result of a numerous of corporate scandals that shook the countries developed or developing alike. Obscure companies quickly listed on the exchanges during the stock market boom of 1993-94 only to disappear after exploiting public funds and leaving the retail investors with illiquid stock. The sudden appearance of fly-by-night operators during the period coupled with the emergence of a new breed of shareholders like the foreign investors, institutional investors, mutual funds and private equity placement companies and their demands for better governance practices has compelled the policy-makers to think of the governance anomalies in corporate India.

Before the onset of liberalization the Indian organized sectors both by public and private enterprises did not meet the expected norms and standards of governance. Both the public and the private sector enterprises were strengthening themselves to meet the challenges of globalization. Moreover, with increasing foreign investment in Indian industries, accountability to foreign shareholders also had become an increasing necessity. Varied opinions were articulated in India in response to wide ranging corporate scandals like violations of foreign exchange regulations, making surreptitious payments to politicians, involvement in illegal activities and unethical deals by the top industrial houses.

In the Indian context, the need for the study of corporate governance has been highlighted because of the scams occurring frequently since the emergence of the concept of liberalization from 1991, such as the Harshad Mehta Scam, Ketan Parikh Scam, UTI Scam, Bhansali Scam and so on. In the Indian corporate scene, there is a need to induct global standards to reduce the scope for scams to the minimum. In this context the paper focuses on the following objectives:

- To have an overview of the events at Enron (American company) and Satyam Computers (Indian company) as a model, that have caused so much trauma and panic throughout the corporate world.
- To study the similarities in Enron and Satyam scams and list out common causes that lead to the above said scams.

Descriptive research methodology has been used to analyse the corporate governance issues existing in the corporate business world and two cases were observed as a sample to recommend the measures to inbuilt corporate governance in the organization structure of all corporations.

ENRON

An Issue of Corporate Governance

Enron was America's energy based company founded in the year 1985. It was formed by merger between two well established brands Houston natural gas and Ohama-based Internorth Inc. It decided to expand its bases further in late 1980s and early 1990 at the places like UK Europe, South America and India. In 1999 it launched its' broadband service unit and Enron online. Over time, eventually, Enron claimed 90 per cent of its trades through Enron online. In August 2000, Enron claimed all time high with profits of more than US $90.

However, February 2001 reported to be the start of Enron's downfall. It had increased on its debt levels to $37.7 billion which was almost 91 per cent higher compared to previous 12 months period. Inspite of this, Enron assets increased to 19.03 per cent. Eventually Enron's market tumbled down to $8.9 billion that is 26 per cent drop in just one week. Its asset volatility remained to 20 per cent. In November, Enron reported that it overstated its earnings dating back to 1997 to almost $600 million. On 9th November 2001, the company reported to deal with its smaller rival Dynegy Inc. to buy Enron's stock at $9 billion. Chevron Texaco agreed to inject $1.5 billion fresh capital immediately. Enron then disclosed that a deterioration of its credit ratings could accelerate repayment of the $690 million loan. However, major credit rating agencies downgraded its bonds and as a result Dynegy terminated to buy Enron. Enron temporarily suspended all its payments other than those necessary to maintain core operations. In December 2001, Enron finally filed for Chapter 11 bankruptcy and hit Dynegy with a $10 billion breach of contract lawsuit.

SATYAM COMPUTERS

Issue of Corporate Governance

In one of the the biggest frauds in India's corporate history, B.Ramalinga Raju, founder and CEO of Satyam Computers, India's fourth-largest IT services firm, announced on January 7 year that his company had been falsifying its accounts for years, overstating revenues and inflating profits by $1 billion. Ironically, Satyam means "truth" in Sanskrit, but Raju's admission of guilt showed that the company had been feeding investors, shareholders, clients and employees a steady diet of *asatyam* (untruth), at least regarding its financial performance.

Raju admitted the fraud of his aborted attempt to have Satyam invest $1.6 billion in Maytas Properties and Maytas Infrastructure ("Maytas" is Satyam spelled backwards)—two firms promoted and controlled by his family members. On December 16, 2008 Satyam's board cleared the investment, sparking a negative reaction by investors, who pummeled its stock on the New York Stock Exchange and Nasdaq. The board hurriedly reconvened the same day and called off the proposed investment.

Resigning as Satyam's chairman and CEO, Raju said in a letter addressed to his board, the stock exchanges and the market regulator Securities and Exchange Board of India (SEBI) that Satyam's profits were inflated over several years to "unmanageable proportions" and that it was forced to carry more assets and resources than its real operations justified. He took sole responsibility for those acts. Specifically, Raju acknowledged that Satyam's balance sheet included Rs. 7,136 crore (nearly $1.5 billion) in non-existent cash and bank balances, accrued interest and misstatements. It had also inflated its 2008 second quarter revenues by Rs. 588 crore ($122 million) to Rs. 2,700 crore ($563 million), and actual operating margins were less than a tenth of the stated Rs. 649 crore ($135 million).

The outrage over Raju's admission of systematic accounting fraud has broadened to wider concern about the potential damage to India's appeal for foreign investors and the IT services industry in particular. Immediately following Raju's confession, Satyam's shareholders took a direct hit as the company's share price crashed 77 per cent to Rs. 30 (approximately 60 cents), a far cry from its 52-week high of Rs. 544 ($11.35) May, 2009. Even as Raju is widely blamed for unleashing "India's Enron".

ENRON *vis-a-vis* SATYAM

Based on the evidences exposed in Enron Scam and Satyam Scam issues, it is observed that mostly very similar factors prevailed in both the cases. Those factors are briefly elucidated in the following lines.

Fiduciary Failure

The Enron Board of Directors failed to safeguard Enron shareholders and contributed to the collapse of the seventh largest public company in the United States. The Board witnessed numerous indications of questionable practices by Enron management over several years, but chose to ignore them to the detriment of Enron shareholders, employees and business associates.

Several institutional investors and sections of the media questioned the action of the Board of Satyam regarding the rationale for diversification of an information technology company into real estate sector and the rationale for paying huge amount of consideration for acquiring stakes in the entities owned by the promoter group, that ultimately lead to its collapse. The ongoing investigations into the Satyam scam which made news early in 2009, showed that all not a single member on the board of directors opposed the fraud that the company was engaging in. The scam robbed investors of around 14,000 crores went unopposed even as the managing directors and owners of the company walked away with 2,700 crores. Investigations show that several top level directors are also guilty of fraud.

Conflicts of Interest

Despite clear conflicts of interest, the Enron Board of Directors approved an unprecedented arrangement allowing Enron's Chief Financial Officer to establish and operate the LJM private equity funds which transacted business with Enron and profited at Enron's expense. The one common denominator behind the corporate failure and fraud in Satyam scam was the lack of effective risk management practice and the indifferent role of the Board of Directors.

In both the cases, Board exercised inadequate oversight of transactions and compensation controls and failed to protect shareholders from unfair dealing.

Oversight of Capital Market Indicators

The capital market of a country indicates ups and downs of the securities traded, the sudden and surprising hikes in the share prices or derivative prices to an unimaginable extent, did not catch the attention of the inspectors of governing body. The impact of Enron's collapse was both profound and widespread as its share price plunged from a 52-week high of $43 on August 13, to less than $1 by the end of 2001.

Following the similar drammatical pattern, immediately after Raju's confession, Satyam's shareholders took a direct hit as the company's share price crashed 77 per cent to Rs. 30 (approximately 60 cents), a far cry from its 52-week high of Rs. 544 ($11.35) May, 2009. Even Raju is widely blamed for unleashing "India's Enron".

Auditors

The role of auditors in manipulating the facts and figures in the financial statements was there to a great extent by unethical compromises, due to financial ties between the company, certain Board members and the company's auditors. It is observed that in both the issues professional malpractice of the accounting standards has been indulged.

Nepotism

There was a clear evidence of nepotism in Enron case by Dr. Wendy Gramm, and in Satyam case by Ramalinga Raju. They misused nepotism concept for settlement of merger and acquisition strategies along with their family members for their sheer personal benefit.

Political Power

In both the cases political parties and their administrative mechanism favoured to empower the scammers and intentionally they ignored unlawful and unethical practices of the culprits.

Governing Body

SEC of America and SEBI of India played the role of nominal regulators at the cost of corporate governance and no proper control mechanism is exerted upon the deliberate violation of the regulatory rules by the Enron and Satyam respectively.

Shareholders

High risk-high return is a well known trading principle. The stake holders assumed win-win mechanism as far as returns are concerned and ignored innate risk, they ventures with. The capital gain of trading activities with an unimaginable profit margins and insider trading as well as lame duck activities are ignored even by experienced shareholders.

It is inferred from the study that the Corporate Governance failure can be attributed to the ineffective management of the board by high risk accounting, inappropriate conflict of interest transactions, extensive undisclosed off-the-books activities, and excessive executive compensation as soft bribing, overstating the profits and manipulation of accounting standards and in lack of transparency in corporate business activities. Overall, it has been observed that the other major lacuna in the modern so-called professional financial world is lack of ethical and moral values. Many more Enrons and Satyams may continue to erupt till we recognize and deal with the true source of the problem. The lasting solution to the problem lies in a transformation of human consciousness though an inner discipline first and it should be the rule for the entire corporate world that "somebody has to watch and somebody has to watch the watchers."

Conclusion

Studies since 1997 have indicated that corporate governance would have resulted even better results if there are sound institutions in the country such as those related to the financial system, competition and ownership structures etc. The new vision for corporate governance arises from the current and future need to reform and strengthen institutions that support and facilitate corporate governance and establishing robust linkage to development challenges. Professional bodies have been among the most active reputation agents in leading the corporate governance charge. Attention should be focused to put forward new strategies to curb anti-corporate governance activities by vesting the power of control in the hands of stakeholders who are the true witness of performance of a company.

References

1. Bajaj. R. Chairman (1997), *Draft code on corporate governance*, Confederation of Indian Industry.
2. Balasubramaniam, N., "Towards Excellence in Board Performance", *The IIMB Management Review*, January-March, 1997, pp. 67-84.
3. Barua, S. K. and Varma, J. R., "FERA in Reverse Gear; MNCs Strike Gold", *Economic Times*, November 12, 1993.
4. Barua, S. K. and Varma, J. R., "MNCs Must be Subjected to SEBI Acquisition Code", *Economic Times*, November 17, 1993.
5. Cadbury, A., Chairman, (1992), *Report on the Financial Aspects of Corporate Governance*.
6. King, M. E., Chairman (1997), *Report on Insider Trading*.
7. Pound, J, "The fight for good governance", *Harvard Business Review*, January-February, 1993, pp.76-83.
8. Pozen, R.C., "Institutional Investors: Reluctant Activists", *Harvard Business Review*, January-February, 1994, pp.140-149.
9. Salmon, W.J., "Crisis Prevention: How to Gear up Your Board", *Harvard Business Review*, January-February, 1994, pp.68-75.
10. Smith, A., "An Inquiry into the Nature and Causes of the Wealth of Nations", *Modern Library Edition*, New York, Random House.
11. Vittal, N., "Boards and Directors in Public Sector Enterprises", *The IIMB-Management Review*, January-March, 1997, pp. 48-56.
12. Reddy, YRK, "Corporate Governance–Directions for the Next Decade", *Vidwat—The Indian Journal of Management*, Vol. 2, Issue 2, July-December, 2009.

Corporate Governance Practices in India

Tatikonda Neelakantam
G. Radha Krishna Murthy
K. Shyamala Devi

ABSTRACT

This study describes the Indian corporate governance system and examines how the system has both supported and held back India's ascent to the top ranks of the world's economies. Corporate governance means maximizing long term shareholders value in a legal, transparent and ethical manner, ensuring fairness, courtesy and dignity in all transactions within and outside the company. Corporate governance provides the fundamental value framework for the culture of an organization, which ensures efficient functioning of enterprises on sound ethical values and principles. Broadly, It is a system of structuring, operating and controlling a company with a view to achieve long term strategic goals to satisfy shareholders, creditors, employers, customers and complying with the legal and regulatory requirements, apart from meeting environmental and local community needs. It defines and confines the rights and responsibilities of the constituents of the corporate like boards, managers, shareholders and other stakeholders. This paper focuses on the practices adopted by India for implementing the corporate governance policies.

Keywords: Corporate Governance, Creditors, Shareholders, etc.

Introduction

This paper describes the Indian corporate governance system and examines how the system has both supported and held back India's ascent to the top ranks of the world's economies. Corporate governance means maximizing long term shareholders value in a legal, transparent and ethical manner, ensuring fairness, courtesy and dignity in all transactions within and outside the company. Corporate governance provides the fundamental value framework for the culture of an organization, which ensures efficient functioning of enterprises on sound ethical values and principle. Corporate governance and economic development are intrinsically linked, particularly as the world economy struggles for equilibrium while stagnant markets and subdued trade dynamics lead to fewer jobs and investments. Before the global financial crisis, India had been making dramatic increases in the scale and distribution of wealth. Liberalization of the economy in 1991 and the move toward globalization sparked the growth of a strong investor culture. Coincidentally, concerns over corporate scandals have helped boost wide-ranging changes in legislation and regulations, resulting in a positive transformation of the corporate sector and the corporate governance landscape. Despite these advances there are still substantial areas that are far from reaching the international best-practices level.

Corporate governance is needed to create a corporate culture of consciousness, transparency and openness. It refers to combination of laws, rules, regulations, procedures and voluntary practices to enable the companies to maximize the shareholders, long-term value. It should lead to increasing customer satisfaction, shareholder value and wealth. It is integral to the very existence of a company. Good corporate governance increases the confidence of investors and results in development of capital market. It strengthens investor's trust and ensures a long-term partnership that helps in fulfilling the company's quest for higher growth and profit. Corporate governance provides directions for business performance; long-term strategy and vision; control and reporting system; and the parameters of accountability. The ultimate purpose of corporate governance is to create a self-driven, self-assessed and self-regulated organization. The issue of corporate governance became particularly significant in the context of globalization because one special feature of the late 20th century/21st century globalization is that in addition to the traditional three elements of the economy, namely physical capital in terms of plant and machinery, technology and labor, the volatile element of financial capital invested in the emerging markets and in the third world countries is an important element of modern globalization and has become particularly powerful. The significance and the impact of the volatility of the financial capital was realized when in June 1997 the currency of Southeast Asian countries started melting down in countries like Thailand, Indonesia, South Korea and Malaysia. It was realized by the World Bank and all investors that it is not enough to have good corporate management but one should have also good corporate governance because the investors want to be sure that the decisions taken are ultimately in the interests of all stakeholders. Honesty is the best policy is a fact that is now being re-discovered. Corporate governance succeeded in attracting a good deal of public interest because of its apparent importance for the economic health of corporations and society in general. Different people have come up with different definitions that basically reflect their special interests in the field. Some of the important and comprehensive definitions of corporate governance are mentioned as under:

Goldberg and Desai defined "Corporate governance is the entire system of rewards, sanctions, co-ordination and conflict-resolution mechanisms used to order and arbitrate the economic interests of shareholders, lenders, managers and employees".

Objectives of the study

- To know the practices of Corporate Governance in India.

- To measure and improve the quality of corporate governance.
- To draw the conclusions and offer suggestions.

Legal and Regulatory Frameworks in India

Red tape and regulations are among the leading deterrents for business and foreign investment in India, leading to its latest ranking of 116 out of 155 in the World Bank's Ease of Doing Business, 2006 publication. India consistently places in the bottom half of the sample for all aspects of business regulation (and is out of the top 100 for most aspects), except for investor protection. Starting a business in India is a monumental operation. Compared to their counterparts in OECD countries, India's entrepreneurs must follow twice the number of procedures, face about three and a half times the time delay, and close to nine times the cost as a proportion of per capita income. Delays and costs of dealing with licenses in India are also far higher than in OECD countries. It is almost twice as hard to hire people in India as in OECD countries, and almost three times as hard and costly to fire them. There is considerable variation in labor laws across Indian states, and Timothy Besley and Robin Burgess show that during the three and half decades before liberalization began in 1991, Indian states that followed more "pro-worker" policies experienced lower output, investment, employment and productivity in the registered or formal sector, as well as higher urban poverty and increased informal sector output.

Enforcement of corporate laws remains the soft underbelly of India's legal and corporate governance systems. The World Bank's 2004 Reports on the Observance of Standards and Codes (ROSC) finds that while India observes or largely observes most of the principles, it could do better in many areas, including the use of nominee directors, the enforcement of laws and regulations pertaining to stock listing on major exchanges, insider trading, and dealing with violations of the Companies Act. Some of these problems arise because of unsettled questions about jurisdictional issues and powers of the SEBI.

Recent Observations

A recent study finds that, during 1997-2002, the average (of a sample of 462 manufacturing firms) board compensation in India has been around Rs. 5.3 million (approximately US $120,000), with wide variation across firm size. The average board compensation is Rs. 7.6 million (US $171,000) for large firms and Rs. 2.5 million (US $56,000) for small firms. The board compensation also appears to be higher, on average, at Rs. 6.9 million (US $155,500) if the CEO is related to the founding family. Both board and CEO compensation depend on current performance, and CEO pay depends on past-year performance as well. Diversified companies also pay their boards more. Given that almost two-thirds of the top 500 Indian companies are group-affiliated, issues relating to corporate governance in business groups are naturally very important. Tunneling, or "the transfer of assets and profits out of firms for the benefit of those who control them" is a major concern in business groups with pyramidal ownership structure and inter-firm cash flows. Marianne Bertrand and her coauthors estimate that an industry shock leads to a 30 per cent lower earnings increase for business group firms compared to stand-alone firms in the same industry. They find that firms farther down the pyramidal structure are less affected by industry-specific shocks than those nearer the top, suggesting that positive shocks in the former are siphoned off to the latter, benefiting the controlling shareholders but hurting the minority shareholders. However, Bernard Black and Vikramaditya Khanna question how this logic would make them less sensitive to negative shocks. There is also some evidence that firms associated with business groups have superior performance than stand-alone firms. More recently Raja Kali and Jayati Sarkar argue that diversified business groups help increase the opacity of within-group fund flows driving a wider wedge between control and cash flow rights. A greater degree of diversification also aids tunneling. Using data for Indian firms in 385 business groups in 2002-03 and 384 groups in 2003-04, Kali and Sarkar find that firms with greater ownership opacity and a lower wedge between cash flow rights and control than those in a group's core activity are likely to be located farther away from the core activity. This incentive for tunneling explains, according to them, the persistence of value destroying groups in India and occasional heavy investment by Indian groups in businesses with low contribution to group profitability. Using a sample of over 600 of the 1000 largest (by revenues) Indian firms in 2004, Jayashree Saha finds that, after controlling for other corporate governance characteristics, firm performance is negatively associated with the extent of related party transactions for group firms but positively so for stand-alone companies. This further strengthens the circumstantial evidence of tunneling and its adverse effects. The same study also reveals that, using a sample of over 5000 firms for the period 2003-2005, most related party transactions in India occur between the firm and "parties with control," as opposed to management personnel as in the United States. Also, group companies consistently report higher levels of related party transactions than stand-alone companies. Transparency and corporate governance levels are very closely related. Cross-country studies have repeatedly put India among the worst nations in terms of earnings capacity and management. Indian accounting standards provide considerable flexibility to firms in their financial reporting and differ from the International Accounting Standards (IAS) in several ways that often make interpreting Indian financial statements a challenging task. These deviations, however, need to be viewed in the right perspective. India still falls short of the median number of deviations from IAS in the 49 country sample of Kee-Hong Bae and co-authors. The nature of corporate governance can affect the capital structure of a company. In the presence of well functioning financial institutions, debt can be a disciplining mechanism in the hands of shareholders or an expropriating mechanism in the hands of controlling insiders. Studying the relationship between leverage and Tobin's Q in 1996, 2000, and 2003, Jayati Sarkar and Subrata Sarkar conclude that the disciplinary effect has been more marked in recent years as institutions have adopted greater market orientations. They also find limited evidence of the use of debt as an expropriating mechanism in group companies. The market for corporate control was relatively limited in India until the mid-1990s, when the average number of mergers per year leapt from 30 between 1973-74 and 1987-88, and 63 between 1987- 88 and 1994-95, to 171 between 1994-95 and 2002-03. Merger activity appears to occur in waves and is split roughly evenly between inter-industry and intra-industry mergers. The share of group-affiliated mergers has increased significantly in the post-1994-95 period. With regard to public sector governance, Nandini Gupta finds that even when control stays in government hands, partial privatization has a positive impact on profitability, productivity, and investment of the PSEs concerned. She argues that the monitoring role of the markets has been responsible for this. Another study argues that the effect of partial privatization may have been confounded with the application of MoUs to these cases before the partial privatizations, finding that the application of MoUs or performance contracts has had a positive impact on profitability as well as operational performance of PSEs.

Suggestions

Although changes in company law, corporate accounting, disclosure norms, setting up audit committees, responsibilities and powers of the board of directors etc. have been recommended for improving corporate governance in India yet some more efforts are also required in this direction. The respondents covered in this study were also of the same opinion. Some fruitful suggestions for the corporate sector, financial institutions, professional bodies, and government have been also quoted in the table 2.1.

Conclusion

With the recent spate of corporate scandals and the subsequent interest in corporate governance, a plethora of corporate governance norms and standards have sprouted around the globe. In the last few years the thinking on the topic in india

Table 2.1: Suggestions to improve corporate governance

Imperatives for Corporate Sector	1. Awarding of Contracts. 2. Transfer Pricing. 3. Use of Company Resources . 4. Presence of Shareholders in Annual General Meeting. 5. Improving Corporate Reputation 6. Formation of Additional Board Committees. 7. Introduction of Cumulative Voting System. 8. Strong Interface between Industry and Academia. 9. Training for Directors. 10. Business Judgment Rule.
Measures for Financial Institutions	1. Financial institutions must take active part in their respective companies. 2. FIs should nominate professionally qualified persons as representatives on the companies' boards. 3. Nominated members of BOD should be made accountable for any mis governance. 4. Institutional investors should made positive use of their voting rights.
Suggestions for Professional and Professional Bodies	1. Peer Review. 2. Audit firm Rotation.
Recommendations for the Government	1. Separate body for Regulating Corporate Governance. 2. Changes in Company Act.

has gradually crystallized into the development of norms for listed companies. The problem for private companies, that form a vast majority of Indian corporate entities, remains largely unaddressed. The agency problem is likely to be less marked there as ownership and control are generally not separated. Minority shareholder exploitation, however, can very well be an important issue in many cases. Development of norms and guidelines are an important first step in a serious effort to improve corporate governance. The bigger challenge in India, however, lies in the proper implementation of those rules at the ground level. More and more it appears that outside agencies like analysts and stock markets (particularly foreign markets for companies making GDR issues) have the most influence on the actions of managers in the leading companies of the country. But their influence is restricted to the few top (albeit largest) companies. More needs to be done to ensure adequate corporate governance in the average Indian company. Even the most prudent norms can be hoodwinked in a system plagued with widespread corruption. Nevertheless, with industry organizations and chambers of commerce themselves pushing for an improved corporate governance system, the future of corporate governance in India promises to be distinctly better than the past.

References

1. Duff, C., John D., and Joann L., (1995), "Kmart's Embattled CEO Resigns Post Under Pressure from Key Shareholders," *The Wall Street Journal*, 3.
2. Johan, A. {Byrne, (1998), "At Least Chainsaw Al Knew How to Hire a Board," *Business Week*, 40.
3. Carroll, Archie B., and Buchholz Ann K., (2000), *"Business and Society: Ethics and Stakeholder Management"* Fourth Edition, South-Western College Publishing, NewYork.
4. Magdi, R. {Iskander and Chamlou, N., (2000), *Corporate Governance: A Framework for Implementation*, 10.
5. Ray, Ghosh, {K., (2001), "Corporate Governance and Reporting Practices in India: A Study", *Management and Change*, 5(2): 423-442.
6. www.sebi.org.
7. Balasubramaniam, N., (1998), *Corporate Governance: Realities and Reforms*, Sterling Publishers Private Limited, New Delhi, p. 183.
8. Compendium on Training Programme of Senior Technical Assistance on *"Company Law in India: Issues and Perspectives"*, (2003). issued by ICAI, DCA, Ministry of Law, Justice and Company Affairs, 73.

9. "Icra Begins Governance Rating with ITC", (2001), *Rating Update, A Periodical Update on Credit Rating,* 1.

10. "Crisil Rates Four Firms on Governance and Value Creation", (2003), *Business Standard,* 6.

11. Gunasingh, D.S., (2003), "Requirement of a Separate Body in India for Regulating Corporate Governance", *The ICFAI Journal of Corporate Governance,* II (2), 82-87.

12. Sridhar, J., (2001), "SEBI's Role in Enhancing the Image of Indian Corporate Sector", *Chartered Secretary,* 869-877.

13. Lyengar, J., (2000), "Greater Disclosures in DCA's New Report", *The Economic Times,* 5.

14. Postlnieu, A., (2003), "NYSE Moves to Improve Governance", *Financial Times,* 7.

15. "Nasdaq Takes Concerted Action" (2002), *Fortune India,* 54-55.

16. Rangarajan, C., (2000), "Corporate Governance the New Paradigm", *The Banker,* 28-31.

17. Jalan, B., (2003), "Corporate Governance: A Key Issue in Banking", *The Financial Express,* 1.

18. www.corpgov.net.

19. Magdi, R. Iskander, Nadereh Chamlou, (2000), "Corporate Governance: A Framework for Implementation", 10.

Tyco International Ltd.

*A long story of governance complacency and fraud**

Prof. Sreejesh S

ABSTRACT

This case study highlights the corporate governance practices of Tyco International Ltd., during the Dennis Kozlowski's tenure (CEO, from 1992 to 2001), and subsequent changes set out by Edward D. Breen (CEO, since 2002) to undo the damage of the Kozlowski era. This case study explores the two assignment questions: What role did Tyco's corporate culture play in the scandal? What roles did the board of directors, CEO, CFO and legal counsel play? Have Tyco's recent actions after the scandal been sufficient to restore confidence in the company? What other actions should the company take to demonstrate that it intends to play by the rules? This case study aimed with two pedagogical objectives: First to explain the Board of Director's and top management's responsibilities (especially CEO and CFO) as a fiduciary and its failures in three areas candor and disclosure, diligence and care and loyalty and self-restraint. Second to explain the changes in governance system carried

*The case was written and compiled from published sources, and is intended to be used as basis for class discussion rather than to illustrate either effective or ineffective handling of a management solution.

out by the successors of top management to restore the fiduciary responsibilities. Third, discuss the actions carried out by the successors of top management to ensure the scandal would not happen again in Tyco International's future.

Keywords: Corporate governance, fiduciary responsibilities, candor and disclosure, diligence and care, loyalty and self restraint.

"I am absolutely not guilty of the charges brought upon me. There was no criminal intent here. Nothing was hidden. There were no shredded documents. Nobody was told not to say anything. All the information the prosecutors got was directly off the books and records of the company."

"I was a guy sitting in a courtroom who made $100 million a year. And I think a juror sitting there just would have to say, 'All that money, he must done something wrong'. I think it's as you know, it's as simple as that."[1]

—Dennis Kozlowski
Former CEO, Tyco International Ltd.

I venture to assert that when the history of the financial era which has just drawn to a close comes to be written, most of its mistakes and its major faults will be ascribed to the failure to observe the fiduciary principle.... No thinking (person) can believe that an economy.... can permanently endure without some loyalty to that principle.[2]

Harlan Fiske Stone
Justice, US Surpreme Court, 1934
Commenting on the events leading to
the Securities Acts of 1933 and 1934

Introduction

In January 2002, the Securities and Exchange Commission (SEC) started an investigation regarding the Corporate Governance practices of Tyco International Ltd. This is started because of the questioning of the accuracy of Tyco's bookkeeping and accounting practices that came under criticism after a tip drew attention to a $20 million payment made to Tyco director Frank Walsh Jr. That payment was later explained as a finder's fee for the Tyco acquisition of CIT. In June 2002, Kozlowski was being investigated for tax evasion because he failed to pay sales tax on $13 million in artwork that he had purchased in New York with company funds.[3] At the same time, Kozlowski resigned from Tyco "for personal reasons" and was replaced by John Fort. Inquiries into the accuracy of the company's books began in January. As investigations continued it was uncovered that Dennis Kozlowski, Tyco's former CEO; Mark Swartz, Tyco's former CFO; and Mark Belnick, the company's chief legal officer, had taken over $170 million in loans from Tyco without receiving appropriate approval from Tyco's compensation committee and notifying shareholders.

Kozlowski and Schwartz are also accused of issuing bonuses to themselves and other employees without approval of Tyco's board of directors. It is alleged that these bonuses acted as *de facto* loan forgiveness for employees who had borrowed company money or were used to buy the silence of those who suspected the former CEO and CFO of fraud. According to Tyco, the individuals who received loan forgiveness were not aware that they were participating in anything illegal; they were told the program had the board's approval. Tyco and the SEC say it did not.[4]

In September 2002, all three executives (Kozlowski, Swartz, and Belnick) were gone and charges were filed against them for failure to disclose information regarding the loan to shareholders. For the most part these loans were taken with low to no interest. Many of them were offset as bonuses without open approval. Kozlowski and Swartz also sold seven and a half million shares of Tyco stock for $430 million without telling investors. Formal charges were made by the SEC September 12, 2002. The SEC asked Kozlowski, Swartz, and Belnick to restore funds they took from Tyco in various forms of undisclosed loans and compensations. Kozlowski and Swartz are charged with: Corruption, conspiracy and falsifying records and Belnick is charged with: Falsifying business reports and failing to disclose loans made to himself (for the purchase of his Manhattan apartment and Utah home), to investors and Tyco's compensation committee Bee Exhibit I.

Exhibit I: Investigations and indictments[5]

Year	Investigations and indictments
January 2002	• Questions rise about the accuracy of Tyco's bookkeeping and accounting. Stock value drops 19 per cent.
January 29, 2002	• Kozlowski explains that the $20 million paid to Frank Walsh was a finder's fee for the acquisition of CIT.
January 30, 2002	• Kozlowski announces that he and Mark Swartz (Tyco's then CFO) will each purchase 500,000 Tyco shares on the open market. This move is made as an assurance of the value of Tyco stock.
April 25, 2002	• Kozlowski explains a 96 per cent loss per share for the quarter ending on March 31, 2002 and outlines unusual costs that affected earnings.
June 3, 2002	• Kozlowski resigns as CEO of Tyco for personal reasons. John Fort is named the temporary CEO.
June 4, 2002	• Kozlowski is indicted for attempted tax evasion.
June 10, 2002	• Belnick, who was hired on to Tyco in 1998 as its chief legal officer, is fired.
June 17, 2002	• Tyco, through the law firm of Boies, Schiller & Flexner, begins the process of suing Belnick for breach of fiduciary duty and fraud. Belnick maintains that he acted wtih integrity as Tyco's chief legal officer.
August 1, 2002	• CFO Swartz resigns from Tyco.
September 12, 2002	• Civil charges are filed against Kozlowski, Swartz, and Belnick by the SEC for failure to disclose to shareholders information on the multi-million dollar loans they borrowed from Tyco.

(Contd...)

September 19, 2002	• Kozlowski is freed on $100 million bail. The bail is paid with a $100 million bond and secured with $10 million in assets from Kozlowski's ex-wife.
	• Swartz is freed on $50 million bail. The bail is paid with a $50 million bond and secured with 500,000 of Swartz's personal Tyco stock Belnick is freed on a $1 million bond.

DENNIS KOZLOWSKI —Most Aggressive CEO

Kozlowski was born in the rundown industrial city of Newark, New Jersey, in 1946, the son of a police investigator. He worked his way through Seton Hall University and trained as an accountant in 1970 with the conglomerate SCM Corp. After few years he moved to Nashua Corp.—a photocopier manufacturer—as director of audit and analysis. Kozlowski's latent ambition started in 1975, after the meeting with Joseph Gaziano, the then CEO, Tyco International. Gaziano pulled off a half dozen big acquisitions as a CEO during 1973 to 1982. After Gaziano's death, John F. Fort III, get into power as CEO in 1982. Fort rationalized the heaping pile of assets that Gaziano had haphazardly acquired, shifting Tyco's focus from growth to profits. Kozlowski was influenced and trained under both Gaziano and Fort, was a testament not only to the breadth of his talents but to his eagerness to succeed. During this period Kozlowski transformed himself from a number-crunching staff man to crack operating executive. In 1987 under Fort regime Kozlowski become the president and later as chief operating officer. Fort resigned as CEO in the mid-1992 and as chairman a few months later. After that Kozlowski assumed power as CEO in 1992.

When Kozlowski stepped up as CEO in Tyco International he had a keen understanding of Tyco's basic strengths and weaknesses. At that time Tyco was a $3.1 billion company organized into four divisions: Fire protection; valves, pipes, and other flow control products; electrical and electronic components; and packaging materials. Major chunk of revenue comes from volatile commercial construction industry. Kozlowski changed the system from a company that depend upon construction and accelerated its growth by acquiring companies in non-cyclical businesses. For increasing the speed of acquisitions, Kozlowski promoted Mark Swartz to Chief Financial Officer. Swartz joined in Tyco in 1991 from Deloitte & Touche. As a director of merger and acquisitions, Swartz played a major role in the transaction, turning around a key report and analyzing its intricacies in less than 24 hours. Swartz developed an extraordinarily close working relationship with Kozlowski that helped him to become as Tyco's second most powerful executive.

Kozlowski became the personification of the acquisition mania of the 1990s, and assumed the qualities necessary for the task—brutishness, aggressiveness, and a commitment to the accumulation of his own personal wealth. Due to his efforts Tyco's revenues rose by 48.7 per cent a year from 1997 to 2001, five times faster than General Electric's. Analysts argued that he deserved to make more than Jack Welch of GE. He was one of the best-paid CEO's of the decade, compensation rose from $67 million in 1998 to $170 million in 1999.[9] In January, *Business Week* named Kozlowski one of the 25 outstanding managers of the year. He was featured on the cover of the magazine in 2001, lauded for being the "most aggressive CEO" and for his "willingness to test the limits of acceptable accounting and tax strategies."

TYCO INTERNATIONAL LTD.

The Company

Tyco International was started as a research laboratory to conduct experimental work for the U.S. government by Arthur J. Rosenberg, Waltham, Massachusetts, in 1960. Initially it functioned as an investment and holding company. The business was incorporated as Tyco Laboratories, Massachusetts, in 1962, and its focus turned to high-tech materials science and energy conversion products for the commercial sector. In 1964, the company went public, and in 1965 it started acquiring other companies to fill gaps in its development and distribution network by acquiring Mule Battery Products. As a result, Tyco's thrust changed to manufacturing of industrial products.[6] The company listed in NYSE on 1974.

In 1992, Dennis Kozlowski become CEO of Tyco Laboratories Inc., he followed intensive acquisition strategy for the next several years. During the period of 1991 to 2001 the company acquired and merged around thousand companies. The important acquisitions carried out by Tyco Laboratories Inc. 1991 to early 2001 are: Wormald International Limited, Neotecha, Hindle/Winn, Classic Medical, Uni-Patch, Promeon, Preferred Pipe, Kendall International Co., Tectron Tube, Unistrut, Earth Technology Corporation, Professional Medical Products, Inc., Thorn Security, Carlisle, Watts Waterworks Businesses, Sempell, ElectroStar, American Pipe & Tube, Submarine Systems Inc., Keystone, INBRAND, Sherwood Davis & Geck, United States Surgical, Wells Fargo Alarm, AMP, Raychem, Glynwed, Temasa and Central Sprinkler designs.[7] In 1993 the company changed its name from Tyco laboratories Inc. to Tyco International Ltd. The main motive behind the name change was to show the company's global presence.

In 1996, Tyco was added to the Standard & Poor's S&P 500 Composite Index, which consists of the 500 publicly-traded companies in the United States with the largest market capitalization.[8] In 1997, Tyco International Ltd. merged with ADT Limited—a publically traded securities exchange company. At the time of merger Tyco International Ltd., of massachusetts was wholly-owned subsidiary of ADT Limited, and simultaneously ADT changed its name to Tyco International Ltd. After the merger Tyco International Ltd., incorporated into Bermuda where it was headquartered in the colonial capital of Hamilton. During 1999 Tyco acquired two S&P 500 companies in a US $3 billion buyout; the electronics connector manufacturer AMP Inc. and a global leader in materials science, Raychem Corp. (See Exhibit IX: See List of Key Acquisitions: 1965-2002).

Compensation

Tyco's executive compensation and reward system also shows evidence of a corrupt culture, or at least an executive culture that fostered a strong sense of executive entitlement. For example, consider the extraordinary golden parachute deal that Mark Swartz enjoyed. Tyco's directors had considered the CFO so valuable that in 2001 they offered Swartz a retention agreement that would provide him with a windfall if they terminated him for any reason other than a felony. Under the terms of the contract, Swartz would receive a $63 million severance payment plus a payment of $8.5 million in previously restricted stock, plus $1.75 million annually for three years in a consulting contract for which he must work 30 days a year (Hechinger & Zuckerman, 2002). The Tyco directors reportedly signed a similar deal with Kozlowski in 2001. He was to get a $135 million severance payment in addition to a lifetime consulting contract for $3.4 million annually, extending his contract to 2008 and stipulating that he could only be fired if he was charged with a felony (Management Mayhem, 2003). Fortunately, for Tyco, it didn't need to pay up: Kozlowski resigned, thereby voiding the contract, and Swartz was fired in relation to the felony charges. A former Tyco International Ltd. director testified that three special bonuses granted to former top executives L. Dennis Kozlowski and Mark H. Swartz in 1999 and in 2000 weren't approved by the company's compensation committee or its full board of directors. Kozlowski was paid $1.33 million in 2002 salary and $2.72 million in "other" compensation—but no bonus. Other compensation included $649,217 for use and maintenance of an apartment in New York, personal use of cars and aircraft of $107,114, and $430,740 in "personal benefits". Former Chief Financial Officer Mark Swartz, also charged with theft and fraud in New York, was paid $971,122 in annual salary and $1.27 million in other compensation. He also didn't receive a bonus. For Swartz, Tyco reported spending $130,661 for a New York apartment, $100,827 on cars and aircraft, and $39,241 in personal benefits. Under questioning from prosecutors, Peter Slusser, a director at the Bermuda conglomerate from 1997 to 2003, said he never discussed with other directors the possibility of granting millions of dollars in loan forgiveness to Mr. Kozlowski, Tyco's former chief executive, and Mr. Swartz, its former chief financial officer, in 1999 or in 2000. Nor did they discuss granting a special bonus to the two executives in late 2000 related to the sale of the ADT Automotive unit, Mr. Slusser said. Kozlowski and Swartz received $16 million and $8 million, respectively, in unauthorized bonuses in connection with the ADT Automotive sale and that they granted millions of dollars of loan forgiveness to themselves as bonuses without proper authorization.[10] Frank E. Walsh Jr., a Tyco director from 1992 to 2002, said under cross examination from a defense attorney that Tyco's board of directors never voted to approve investment banking or legal fees in his time on the board. That authority was delegated to Mr. L. Dennis Kozlowski, Tyco's chief executive officer. Mr. Kozlowski, without proper authorization from Tyco's board, paid $20 million to Mr. Walsh and a charity of Mr. Walsh's choosing in connection with the acquisition of CIT Group Inc. in 2001. Mr. Walsh later pleaded guilty to securities fraud in the matter.[11] Patricia Prue, the Bermuda conglomerate's vice president of human resources from 1998 to 2002, said an outside attorney for Tyco determined that millions of dollars in cash and stock Mr. Belnick, company's former top lawyer received as a bonus for helping resolve an accounting inquiry by the Securities and Exchange Commission that year shouldn't be used in calculating whether his compensation should be included in its annual proxy. Mr. Belnick also borrowed more than $14.8 million under the company's relocation program, first to buy an apartment near Central Park in Manhattan and later to buy a home in Utah. Mr. Belnick is on trial in New York State Supreme Court in Manhattan, charged with grand larceny, securities fraud and falsifying business records in connection with as much as $32 million in bonuses and loans he received while working at Tyco[12] Patricia Prue, who left Tyco in December 2002. Mark

H. Swartz, the Bermuda conglomerate's former chief financial officer, told her to include only the compensation of L. Dennis Kozlowski, Tyco's ex-chairman and chief executive, Mr. Swartz and Tyco's operating presidents in paperwork presented to the compensation committee prior to their meeting. As a result, Mr. Belnick's compensation and the compensation of Mr. Kozlowski's subordinates other than Mr. Swartz—weren't seen by committee members until 2002.[13]

Board Governance

In Tyco International the board ceded much of its authority to Mr. Kozlowski, including granting him the ability to make acquisitions on Tyco's behalf costing as much as $200 million and to set the compensation of executives who reported directly to him. "In truth, this board was very happy to ride up the Kozlowski elevator in the 1990s," Mr. Reid Weingarten said, a lawyer in the prosecution, "They made a lot of money. They essentially served as a rubber stamp." He again added, Tyco was a fast-growing company "flush with money" that had a loose management style with few centralized controls.[14]

It is becoming increasingly clear that Tyco was not run or structured like any other company. Even as it ballooned to a $36 billion giant with over 200,000 employees, Kozlowski allowed only a relative handful of trusted lieutenants to work with him at Tyco's headquarters operations, TME Management Inc. Tyco's once-heralded lean, mean management structure now looks more like a setup designed to keep out prying eyes. Within his inner sanctum, Kozlowski reigned supreme. He never appointed a president and handpicked his top managers, insuring that they were cut from his own mold: "smart, poor, and wants-to-be-rich," as he once said. But that cunning structure is no excuse for the seemingly willful blindness exercised by other key Tyco players. Indeed, there's plenty of blame to go around in the sorry saga. The most egregious failure of oversight occurred on Tyco's board. True, Kozlowski apparently went to enormous lengths to keep outside directors in the dark. He took control of all information—including internal audits—that usually go to a board. Given that many of Tyco's supposedly independent directors had direct financial dealings with the company, it's little surprise that the board lacked vigilance. One director, for instance, Joshua M. Berman, was receiving $360,000 annually for "legal services," according to SEC filings. But that pales compared with the $20 million fee Kozlowski paid to "lead director" Frank E. Walsh Jr. for his services in helping to arrange Tyco's disastrous 2001 acquisition of commercial-finance company CIT Group.

Although the board of Tyco has said it was unaware of the extravagant pay packages and loans given to the company's top executives, minutes of the board's compensation committee show that group knew of many of the payments for months before the board took steps to disclose them. In addition, a senior Tyco executive told a Manhattan grand jury and the company's lawyers that one board member put pressure on her, unsuccessfully, to try to get her to doctor the minutes of a compensation committee meeting, executives and lawyers involved in the investigations of Tyco said. During that meeting, at least one of the controversial pay packages was approved to make it appear as if there was no such approval, they said. That board member denied the accusation. Tyco had filed a document with the Securities and Exchange Commission saying the investigation found that board members had no knowledge of excessive pay packages for Kozlowski, Swartz and Beilnick.[15]

Timeline of inequity[16]

The problems of inequity in Tyco International started in January 22, 2002, when the company announces its growth strategy that the company plans to break into four pieces. The reason behind the breaking up of the company was to maximize shareholder value. Soon after the announcement of Tyco's new growth strategy, the company again made an announcement that it posed negative free cash flow in the prior quarter. The market reacts negatively to this announcement and stock prices fell down to 50 per cent over the following five weeks and S & P 500 declines by 1 per cent.

In July 2001, Tyco discloses that the cash payment made to the board member Frank Walsh considered as Finder's fee related to CIT acquisition. But the question rose against Walsh, because he was the lead director, a member of the board's corporate governance and nominating committee and a substantial shareholder in CIT. According to the company report the board members did not aware of the $20 million payment to their lead director Walsh. Apparently these payments were made and sanctioned by the CEO with no knowledge from any other director. Realizing the fact that the payment made to the lead director would cause significant objection from shareholders, the board demanded to the lead director to return the cash on January 16, 2002, which Walsh allegedly refused to do.

In February, 2002 Tyco confirms that it had acquired about 700 companies without disclosing the acquisitions in SEC filing that deal is worth about $8 billion. Following this in April, 2002 the company announces that it would abandon the growth plan it had announced in January, and posts a $1.9 billion loss. In June 2002, Kozlowski caught under criminal investigation for suspected tax evasion. Finally it led to the resignation from the post as CEO.

The Aftermath

After Kozlowski's resignation, the board appointed John F. Fort III as interim chief executive officer. Fort was Tyco's lead director and had been CEO from 1982 to1992. In July 2002, the board selected Ed Breen, former president and COO at Motorola, as a permanent CEO of Tyco International Ltd., When Ed Been came into power he had a clear idea about the future governance of Tyco. As part of his new governance structure formation Ed Breen replaced every senior executives of Tyco. It is clear from all activities of Ed that he would insist on the highest standards of business practices and ethics, which helps to create high-quality talent in the organization.

First few months in his office as a CEO, Ed Breen concentrated on three areas: stabilizing operations, restoring investor confidence and compiling cash. He realized the fact that executive suite was not the only place where the cleaning is required (Pillmore, 2002). As part of restoring investor confidence Ed Breen met with a number of larger investors of the company who expressed their strong resentment and replacement of the company's board composition. He decided to change the company from an M&A machine to an operational-driven company, for that the company need different levels of expertise in the board. But replacing a new board was not an easy task as far as new executives of the company concerned. Ed Breen succeeded in convincing the board and finally board decided to step aside. The new board which created, composed of members from all fields of expertise. This ensured a board of governance which is operations literate. In short, the creation of new board was with an orientation toward a philosophy of controllership and accountability. For representing the board the new lead director or non-executive chair, John A. Krol assumed power in 2002, and he told the new CEO, that parts of the business which were chronically underperforming or trapped in commoditizing markets did not belong to Tyco at all. Unlike Kozlowski Ed Breen focused more on consolidating all the Tyco subsidiaries. As part of this consolidation the company started divesting many of the loss-making units, these decisions were made jointly by both CEO and lead Director. One unit—Tycom, producer of undersea cables—was hemorrhaging so much cash (around $300 million annually) that Breen and Krol recommended to the board that it be sold immediately (Useem, 2006).

In 2003 Breen and Krol together prepared a list of 60 companies which were considered to be loss-making units and presented to the board for reviewing its possibility of disposing off. But the directors asked the Breen's team to explain the financial and strategic pros and cons of disposing of each unit. In six cases the board decided that the case for divestiture was not yet conclusive or that the timing was not right. After that Breen, in a public meeting stated that the disposal of units generating 6 per cent of Tyco's revenue.

Ed Breen realized the fact that replacing the board would not provide an ultimate solution to the efficient governance system. Instead the company should make controls robust enough to prevent potential misbehavior within the executive ranks and restore confidence in the board's leadership (Pillmore, 2002). The first step towards this initiative was to put delineations between finance and operations management. As part of that the company put an end to reporting relationship: previously, CFOs reported to the operating bosses of their business segment, but after this these CFOs should report to new corporate CFO directly. This relationship ensured the company to strengthen the checks and balances between finance and operation and everyone in finance department is on the same page. As part of restricting the company's functional strength Ed Breen introduced many initiatives like revitalization of internal audit term. This is mainly done to ensure the independence and objectivity of auditing. To accomplish this objective, the audit function reports directly to the board's audit committee rather than to the CFO.

As part of giving the real control for the board, the company introduced many initiatives. One of the important initiatives of Tyco was that three senior positions within the company's management structure report directly to the board (Pillmore, 2002). First, senior vice-president of corporate governance (which didn't exists before) who should report directly to board's nominating and governance committee, and had a dotted-line relationship to the CEO. Second, corporate ombudsman (which didn't exists before), should report directly to the board's audit committee. The role of ombudsman was to ensure there is a direct, confidential and impartial available to anyone who wants to raise issues about company's compliance with industry regulations (Pillmore, 2002). Their office field covers matters of external constituencies like investors, suppliers, customer and employees. Third, vice-president, corporate audit, also responsible to report the board directly. Another initiative for increasing the effectiveness in the board governance was to establishment of clear principles and policies by which it would operate. For assuring that the company sought advice of two governance experts from Wharton School of Management and Yale School of Management and also studied many of the world's top class companies' governance practices. As part of these initiatives the board got direct control and power for deciding which divisions should stay and which one should go. Tyco International Ltd., drafted a list of 25 good governance practices the company wanted to explore and introduce in the future. For guiding the conduct of employees the company developed a *Guide to Ethical Conduct* for employees, which covered the areas of employee harassment, conflicts of interest, compliance with laws and fraud.

In Ed Breen tenure, Tyco International Ltd., introduced a new compensation structure to help people stay focused and working in concert. The important changes in compensation structure are: *(a)* company introduced bonuses that are contingent upon company performance; the motive behind this initiative was to encourage more corporations among different divisions of the company, *(b)* establishment of an annual bonus plan, *(c)* changes made for the directors compensation—equity part of the directors compensation from stock options to stock units that vest when they retire from the board, *(d)* the company issued some stock-ownership guidelines for management; according to this new rule the senior executives of the company required to keep a minimum percentage of shares acquired through equity awards and, overtime, to hold certain amounts of Tyco common stock, *(e)* started putting a cap on severance payments; according to this new rule senior executives will avail only limited severance (twice of their base salary and bonus) at the time of termination.

Exhibit: II Directors, Officers and Key management in 2001

Directors	*Corporate Officer*
L. Dennis Kozlowski *Chairman of the Board and* *Chief Executive Officer*	**L. Dennis Kozlowski** *President* *Chief Executive Officer*
Lord Ashcroft KCMG *Chairman* *Carlisle Holdings Limited*	**Mark A. Belnick** *Executive Vice-President* *Chief Corporate Counsel*
Joshua M. Berman	**Michael L. Jones** *Secretary*
Richard S. Bodman *Managing General* *Partner Venture* *Management Services Group*	**Mark H. Swartz** *Executive Vice-President* *Chief Financial Officer*
John F. Fort **Stephen W. Foss** *Chairman and Chief Executive* *Officer* *Foss Manufacturing Company, Inc.*	**Business Segment** **Presidents**
Wendy E. Lane *Chairman* *Lane Holdings, Inc.*	**Albert R. Gamper, Jr.** *President* *Tyco Capital*
James S. Pasman, Jr.	**Jürgen W. Gromer** *President* *Tyco Electronics*
W. Peter Slusser *President* *Slusser Associates, Inc.*	**Richard J. Meelia** *President* *Tyco Healthcare*
Mark H. Swartz *Executive Vice-President* *and Chief Financial Officer*	
Frank E. Walsh, Jr. *Chairman* *Sandy Hill Foundation*	
Joseph F. Welch *Chairman and Chief Executive Officer* *The Bachman Company*	

Source: Company Annual Report, Tyco International Ltd.

Exhibit: III Operating Margin

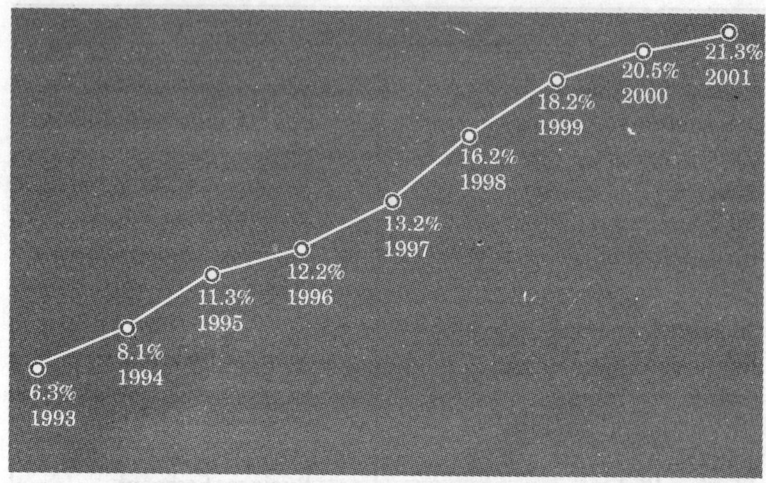

Source: Company Annual Report, Tyco International Ltd.

Exhibit: IV Revenue $ in Billion

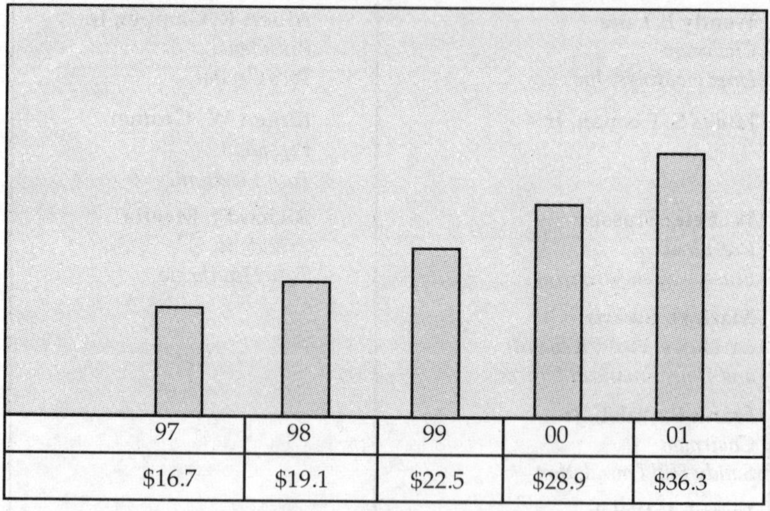

97	98	99	00	01
$16.7	$19.1	$22.5	$28.9	$36.3

Source: Company Annual Report, 2001, Tyco International Ltd.

Exhibit: V Stock Price (Sep. 30, in Dollars Per Share)

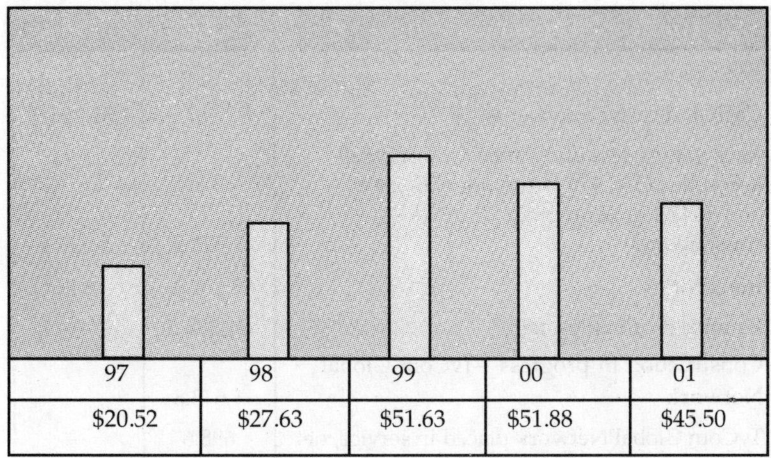

Source: Company Annual Report 2001, Tyco International Ltd.

Exhibit: VI Revenues by Segment

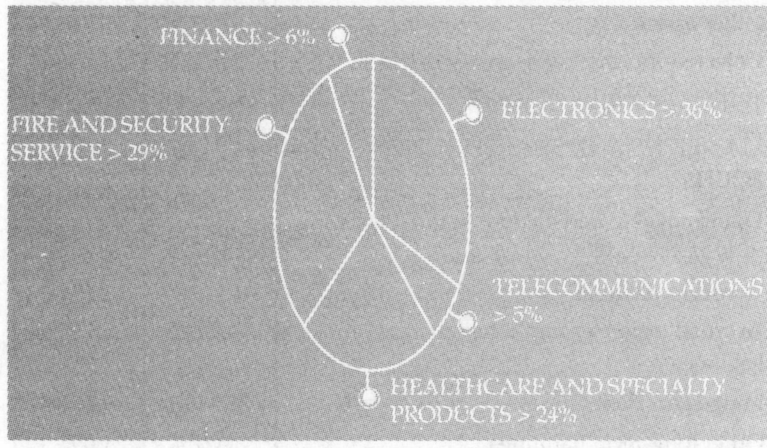

Source: Company Annual Report, 2001, Tyco International Ltd.

Exhibit:VII Consolidated Balance Sheets

Sep 30 (in Million except share data)	2001	2000
ASSETS		
Cash and cash equivalents	$2,587.2	$1,264.8
Receivables, less allowance for doubtful accounts ($550.4 at September 30, 2001 and $442.1 at September 30, 2000 consolidated)	7,372.5	5,630.4
Inventories	5,101.3	3,845.1
Finance receivables, net	31,386.5	—
Construction in progress—TyCom Global Network	1,643.8	—
TyCom Global Network placed in service, net	698.6	—
Property, plant and equipment (including equipment leased to others), net	16,473.9	8218.4
Investment in Tyco Capital	—	—
Goodwill and other intangible assets,net	35,310.4	16332.6
Other assets	8,190.4	3,786.1
Deferred income taxes	2,522.7	1,215.8
TOTAL ASSETS	$111,287.3	$40,404.3
LIABILITIES AND SHAREHOLDERS' EQUITY		
Loans payable and current maturities of long-term debt	$18,873.6	$1,537.2
Accounts payable	4,145.9	3,291.9
Accrued expenses and other current liabilities	10,599.5	5,138.9
Long-term debt	38,243.1	9,461.8
Other long-term liabilities	3,477.4	1,095.3
Income taxes	1,922.7	1,650.3
Deferred income taxes	1,726.3	852.2
TOTAL LIABILITIES	78,988.5	23,027.6

(Contd...)

Commitments and contingencies (Note 22)		
mandatorily redeemable preferred securities	260.0	—
Minority interest	301.4	343.5
SHAREHOLDERS' EQUITY:		
Preference shares	—	—
Common shares (1,935,464,840 and 1,684, 511,070 shares outstanding in 2001 and 2000, respectively)	387.1	336.9
Capital in excess:		
Share premium	7,962.8	5,233.3
Contributed surplus	12,561.3	2,786.3
Accumulated earnings	12,305.7	8,427.6
Accumulated other comprehensive (loss) income	1,479.5	249.1
TOTAL SHAREHOLDERS' EQUITY	31,737.4	17,033.2
TOTAL LIABILITIES AND SHAREHOLDERS' EQUITY	$111,287.3	$40,404.3

Source: Company Annual Reports, 2001, Tyco International Ltd.

Exhibit: VIII Consolidated statement of operations (Tyco International Ltd. and its subsidiaries)

Sep 30 (in Million except share data)	*2001*	*2000*	*1999*
REVENUES			
Net revenue	$34,036.6	$28,931.9	$22,496.5
Finance income	1,676.3	—	—
Other income	334.9	—	—
Earnings of Tyco Capital	—	—	—
Net gain on sale of common shares of subsidiary	64.1	1,760.0	—
Net gain on sale of businesses and investments	276.6	—	—
TOTAL REVENUES	3636,388.5	30,691.9	22,496.5
COSTS AND EXPENSES			
Cost of revenue	20,950.3	17,931.2	14,433.1
Selling, general, administrative and other costs and expenses	7,208.4	5,252.0	4,436.3
Interest and other financial charges, net	1,373.6	769.6	485.6
Provision for credit losses	116.1	—	—
Merger, restructuring and other non-recurring charges, net	233.6	175.3	928.8
Write-off of purchased in-process research and development	184.3	—	—
Charges for the impairment of ong-lived assets	120.1	99.0	507.5
TOTAL COST AND EXPENSES	30,186.4	24,227.1	20,791.3

(Contd...)

INCOME BEFORE INCOME TAXES, MINORITY INTEREST, EXTRAORDINARY ITEMS AND CUMULATIVE EFFECT OF ACCOUNTING CHANGES	6,202.1	6,464.8	1,705.2
Income taxes	1,479.9	1,926.0	637.5
Minority interest	51.1	18.7	—
Income before extraordinary items and cumulative effect of accounting changes	4,671.1	4,520.1	1,067.7
Extraordinary items, net of tax	17.1	0.2	45.7
Cumulative effect of accounting changes, net of tax	683.4	—	—
NET INCOME	$ 3,970.6	$ 4,519.9	$ 1,022.0
BASIC EARNINGS PER COMMON SHARE:			
Income before extraordinary items and cumulative effect of accounting changes	$2.59	$2.68	$0.65
Extraordinary items, net of tax	0.01	—	—
Cumulative effect of accounting changes, net of tax	0.38	—	—
Net Income	2.20	2.68	0.62

(Contd...)

Sep 30 (in Million except share data	2001	2000	1999
DILUTED EARNINGS PER COMMON SHARE:			
Income before extraordinary items and cumulative effect of accounting changes	$2.55	$2.64	$0.64
Extraordinary items, net of tax	0.01	—	—
Cumulative effect of accounting changes, net of tax	0.37	—	—
Net Income	2.17	2.64	0.61
WEIGHTED-AVERAGE NUMBER OF COMMON SHARES OUTSTANDING:			
Basic	1,806.9	1,688.0	1,641.3
Diluted	1,831.6	1,713.2	1,674.8

Source: Annual Report, 2001, Tyco International Ltd.

Exhibit: IX List of key acquisitions (1965-2002)[17]

FY1965 MULE BATTERY PRODUCTS	*FY1974* SIMPLEX WIRE AND CABLE
FY1976 GRINNELL FIRE PROTECTION SYSTEMS	*FY1979* ARMIN CORPORATION
FY1981 LUDLOW CORPORATION	*FY1986* ITT GRINNELL CORPORATION
FY1988 ALLIED TUBE AND CONDUIT	*FY1989* MUELLER COMPANY
FY1991 WORMALD INTERNATIONAL LTD. *FY1994* MODERN INTEGRATED SYS LTD. CLASSIC MEDICAL JAMES RIVER (BONE GUARD) STANLEY FLAGG UNIPATCH PROMEON ENTERPRISE ALL STATE FIRE PROTECTION PREFERRED PIPE NATIONAL FIRE & SECURITY	*FY1993* U-BRAND ROCKFORD WINN/HINDLE IRS *FY1995* SEPCI LMI SHERIDAN KENDALL CAMBREX JJ PIPE INNODOUBLE TECTRON SMITH VALVE

(Contd…)

	DEBRO ENGINEERING CAPITAL FP ENGINEERING LINTOTT UNISTRUT
FY1996	*FY1997*
WAJAX - GAAM	THORN
AUTOMATIC SPRINKLER	MELBOURNE FIRE BRIGADE
RATHGERBER	RJ BRODIE
BELGICAST	SHIELD IND
NEOTECHA GMBH	METALBILT
TRIANGLE	ARBO
PROMED	ROCHESTER
EARTH TECH	WATTS
WHITMAN & HOWARD	CARLISLE
STAR SPRINKLER	UNISTRUT EUROPE
BELL WALKER ENGINEERING	STEEL SUPPORT SYSTEMS
PREFERRED CO2 SYSTEMS	T.J.COPE
SENTRY	ZETTLER
BETHAM	ELECTROSTAR
NASHUA	SEMPELL VALVE GROUP
SANTEX (JV)	AMERICAN TUBE & PIPE
STOCKHAM	DIFFERENT DIMENSIONS INC

(Contd...)

DOOR/HVAC BUSINESSES	PROFESSIONAL FIRE PROTECT CONTOUR MEDICAL PANMEDICA
JULY-SEPT 97	*FY1998*
SSI	WIBORG
ADT	JASON
ARMOURGARD SECURITY LTD	HONEYWELL
PROCLINICS	BUCK
CAMP	DEWRANCE
INBRAND	MICHAEL INDUSTRIES
KEYSTONE	ACROBA
	SANTEX
	INTECVA
	HOLMES PROTECTION
	SHERWOOD
	GUBRI
	FDC ELECT.
	CANTECH CONTROLS
	PROTEX
	NE FIRE
	GANMILL
	CONFAB
	WELLS FARGO ALARM
	SIGMA CIRCUITS
	CIPE

(Contd...)

FY 1999	*FY 2000*
US SURGICAL GRAPHIC CONTROLS SUNBELT PLASTICS ENTERGY SECURITY AMP ALARMGUARD GLYNWED CENTRAL SPRINKLER TEMASA RAYCHEM	GSI AFC SEIMENS PRAEGITZER THOMAS & BETTS
FY2001	*FY2002*
MALLINCKRODT INNERDYNE LUCENT POWER SIMPLEX SCOTT TECHNOLOGIES CIT EDISON SELECT	CAMBRIDGE ALARM (SECURITY SENSORMATIC PARAGON TRADE BRANDS CII TECHNOLOGIES

Assignment Questions

1. What role did Tyco's corporate culture play in the scandal? What roles did the board of directors, CEO, CFO and legal counsel play?

2. Have Tyco's recent actions after the scandal been sufficient to restore confidence in the company? What other actions should the company take to demonstrate that it intends to play by the rules? How the company's top management could ensure it wouldn't happen again?

Pedagogical Objective

This case study aimed with two pedagogical objectives:

1. First to explain the responsibilities of board of directors and top management (especially CEO and CFO) as a fiduciary and its failures in three areas— candor and disclosure, diligence and care and loyalty and self restraint.

2. Second to explain the changes in governance system carried out by the successors of top management to restore the fiduciary responsibilities.

3. Third, discuss the actions carried out by the successors of top management to ensure the scandal would not happen again in Tyco International's future.

Teaching Note

1. *Explain the board of director's and top management's responsibilities (CEO and CFO) as a fiduciary and its failures in three areas— candor and disclosure, diligence and care and loyalty and self restraint?*

Role of Director

- Manage the board and conduct of meetings.
- Good business and financial knowledge.
- Maintain good relations with the Executive directors Independent directors and CEO.

Role of CEO with Respect to the Board

- Good relationship with directors and Chairman.
- Assist the executive directors in presenting the strategic proposals.
- To present the company to the investors.
- To act as a representative of executive directors while interacting with independent directors.

Annexure (TN) 3.1: The Relationship between Board, Top management and Shareholders

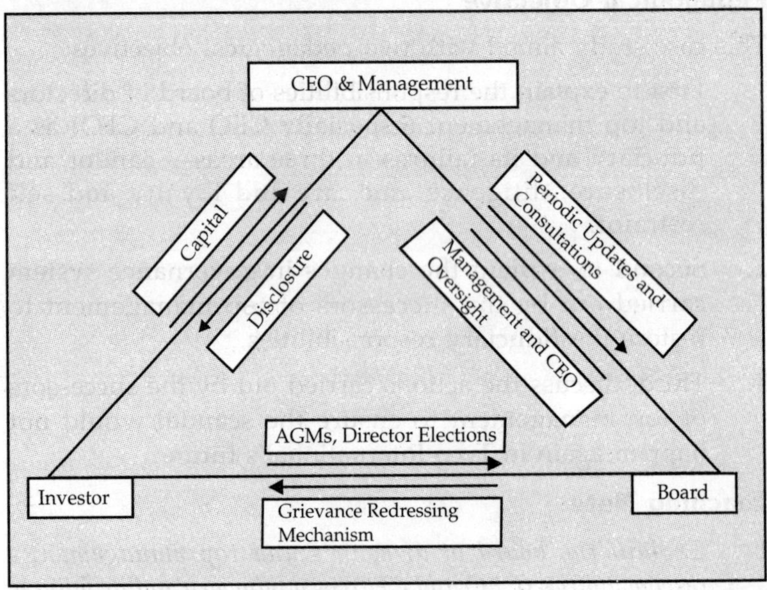

Source: Prepared by the author.

With the help of Annexure 3.1 we can explain the role of three stakeholders of organization in Corporate Governance. The main objective of this case is to explain the fiduciary responsibility of each stakeholder, especially the fiduciary responsibilities of top management and board of directors for the efficient management of corporate governance practices in the organization.

Fiduciary Responsibility

In general, fiduciary relationship arises when a party is entrusted with property, information, or power to make decisions that involve discretionary judgment for the benefit of someone other than himself. In this relationship the trusted party is the fiduciary. In short, a Fiduciary is a person in whom trust and confidence have been reposed and who is under the duty to act for the benefit of another. In the absence of trust and confidence the fiduciary relationship does not exists.

In an organization the executives and board of directors are the fiduciaries for the corporation and its shareholders respectively. In this case the board of directors and top management or executives (CEO & CFO) are responsible for performing the fiduciary duties other than their normal duties as board of directors and executives. So from the case it is evident that these two stakeholders failed to perform their respective duties as fiduciaries.

The special responsibilities of Fiduciaries fall into three categories:

1. *Candor and Disclosure*

In normal contract or arms-length contract the contractual parties are not required to disclose and reveal the facts which are likely to benefit or harm the contract unless and until that is mentioned in the contractor expressly call for such contract, but in fiduciary in similar situation would be obliged to disclose. In many situations the board of directors and top management failed to perform candor and disclosure. (Derive the situations from class discussion).

2. *Diligence and Care*

In ordinary contract or arm's length contract the responsibilities are clearly defined and spelled out in terms of their contract but in fiduciary they are subject to open ended duties to exercise their best efforts on the beneficiary's behalf. For doing so they would exercise diligence, care and skills that are best interest of their corporation. From the past, it is clear that Tyco international's finance department is dealing more with getting deals (hundreds of acquisitions) than with controlling the company's assets. In short, invariably they were far away from the fundamental tasks. From the case it is evident that all most all the acquisitions board of directors did not show any diligence and care. (Derive the situations from class discussion).

3. *Loyalty and self-restraint*

In ordinary contract there is no obligation to protect another party's interest unless that is mentioned in the contract, but in fiduciary not only protect and preserve the beneficiary (corporation and shareholders) interest but also avoid putting their interest ahead of the beneficiary's. But from the case it is evident that in many situations the board of directors and top management failed to perform this responsibility as a fiduciary (Derive situations from the class discussion).

2. *The changes in governance system carried out by the successors of top management to restore the fiduciary responsibilities.*

The important changes carried out by the successors are:

- Replacement of senior executives.
- Concentration on three areas: stabilizing operations, restoring investor confidence and compiling cash.
- Decided to change the company from an M&A machine to an operational-driven company.
- Restructuring of board of directors.
- Appointment of new lead director or non executive chair.
- Decided to dispose off loss making units.
- Creation of delineations between finance and operations management.
- Three senior positions within the company's management structure report directly to the board.
- Introduced a new compensation structure.

3. *Discuss the actions carried out by the successors of top management to ensure the scandal would not happen again in Tyco International's future.*

Many of the action carried out by the new CEO (mentioned above) were in a position that seems to ensure the scandal would not happen in Tyco again and able to restore fiduciary responsibilities in the organization.

- e.g. ongoing dialogue between CEO and the non-executive or lead director.
- Tyco's directors challenged management's reco-mmended set of units for divestiture, altering the final list.
- (Derive more from Class Discussion)

The above are main decision-making primer that ensured the scandal would not happen in Tyco's future.

Annexure (TN)-3.2
Teaching Plan

Sl. No.	*Expected Learning Objectives*	*Learning Objectives*	*Duration in Minutes*
1.	The role of three stakeholders in the organization (Top Management, Board of Directors and Shareholders) especially the role as a fiduciary.	• Role and responsibilities of three stake-holders in CG • fiduciary responsibility.	30
2.	Failure of fiduciary responsibilities.	• Three areas of failure • Candor and disclosure • Diligence and care • Loyalty and self-restraint.	15
3.	Governance changes in Tyco International Ltd.	• Structural changes in governance system carried out by the new CEO (To understand) why did these changes were essential for Tyco)	15
4.	How did these actions carried out by successors of Kozlowski to ensurefiduciary responsibilities.	• Way of restoration and protection of fiduciary responsibilities. • To understand the reason behind the ongoing dialogue between CEO and the non-executive or lead director. • To Understand the reason behind the request and evaluation of explanations and assum-ptions for proposed executive action.	15

Source: Prepared by the Author.

Notes

1 http://blogs.wsj.com/law/2007/03/26/dennis-kozlowski-prisoner-05a4820/

2 Stone, "The public influence of the Bar", 48 Harvard L. Review, (1934), pp.1, 8.

3 http://money.howstuffworks.com/cooking-books10.htm

4 http://www.tycofraudinfocenter.com/information.php

5 http://www.lawyershop.com/practice-areas/criminal-law/white-collar-crimes/securities-fraud/lawsuits/tyco/

6 http://www.tyco.com/wps/wcm/connect/tyco+who+we+are/Who+We+Are/History

7 http://en.wikipedia.org/wiki/Tyco_International

8 Standard and Poor's Corporation (2007). *Standard and Poor's 500 Guide*. New York: McGraw-Hill.

9 Joseph Kay, 18 June 2002, Tyco: US conglomerate falls amid revelations of greed and corruption, *World Socialist Web Site*, published by the International Committee of the Fourth International (ICFI) wsws.org

10 Executives on Trial: "Tyco Witness Says" Pay Lacked Approval; Kozlowski, Swartz Received Millions Without Authority of Board, Witness Testifies *Wall Street Journal* (Eastern edition), New York, N.Y.: Mar 29, 2005 pp. C.3

11 Executives on Trial: "Kozlowski was Cleared to Pay Fees, Says a Former Director at Tyco" *Wall Street Journal* (Eastern edition), New York, N.Y.: Feb 8, 2005. p. C.4

12 Executives on Trial: "Tyco Consulted Outside Attorneys on Disclosing Pay, Witness Says" *Wall Street Journal* (Eastern edition), New York, N.Y.: May 27, 2004 pp. C.5

13 Executives on Trial: "Former Tyco Officer Testifies Belnick Pay Not Seen Before '02" *Wall Street Journal* (Eastern edition), New York, N.Y.: May 26, 2004. pp. C.3

14 Executives on Trial: "Tyco Ex-Lawyer Belnick Believed His Compensation was Approved" *Wall Street Journal* (Eastern edition), New York, N.Y.: Jul 7, 2004 . pp. C.3

15 "Fraud claims continue to mount in Tyco case", Jeff Feingold. *New Hampshire Business Review Concord:* Oct. 04, 2002 Vol. 24, Iss. 21; pp. A22

16 Pascal N. Levensohn, 2005, "Tyco's betrayal of board governance", Board Accountability, summer, pp. 35-38.

17 http://media.corporate-ir.net/media_files/irol/11/112348/reports/tyco_acquisitions.pdf

Additional Readings and References

1. Carcello, Beasley, M. J., and Hermanson, D. "COSO's new fraud study: what it means for CPAs." *Journal of Accountancy,* May, 1999. Find Articles.com.
   http://www.findarticles.com/p/articles/mi_m6280/is_5_187/ai_54636916.
2. Corporate Scandal Primer. *Washington Post.*
   http://www.washingtonpost.com/wp-srv/business/scandals/primer/index.html
3. Domash, Harry. "3 'creative accounting' flags for investors." *MSN Money,* 2005.
   http://moneycentral.msn.com/content/Investing/Simple strategies/P82399.asp?Printer.
4. Donaldson, William H. "SEC Testimony: Impact of the Sarbanes-Oxley Act." Securities and Exchange Commission, April 21, 2005.
   http://www.sec.gov/news/testimony/ts042105whd.htm
5. Elstrom, Peter, "How to Hide $3.8 Billion in Expenses." Business Week Online, June 28, 2002.
   http://www.businessweek.com/bwdaily/dnflash/jun2002/nf20020628_9459.htm.
6. *The Enron Fraud,* http://www.enronfraud.com/
7. Ferraro, S. and C. McPeak. "Managing Earnings...or Cooking the Books?" Graziadio Business Report, Summer 2000.
   http://gbr.pepperdine.edu/003/reporting.html
8. *Howard v. AOL Order*. AOL Legal Department.
   http://legal.web.aol.com/decisions/dlpriv/howardorder.html
9. Jensen, Bob, "*Accounting Scandal Updates and Other Fraud.*" Trinity University, June 30, 2004.
   http://www.trinity.edu/rjensen/fraud063004.htm
10. Katz, David M., "*Pension Plans Underfunded, Says Survey.*" CFO.com, April 1, 2003.
    http://www.cfo.com/article.cfm/3008870?f=related
11. Longley, Robert, "*Enron: Crouching Profits, Hidden Debt.*" About.com.
    http://usgovinfo.about.com/library/weekly/aa011402a.htm
12. Mayer, David, "Leasing 101: What is "Variable Interest Entity?" *Business Leasing News,* February, 2003.
    http://www.pattonboggs.com/Newsletters/Bln/Release/bln_2003_02.htm#6

13. McDonald, Elizabeth, *Tyco's Goodwill Games*. Forbes.com, June 13, 2002.
http://www.forbes.com/2002/06/13/0613tycaccount.html

14. Puplava, Jim, "A Penny Less, A Penny More", *Financial Sense Online: Stormwatch*, November 9, 2001.
http://www.financialsense.com/stormwatch/oldupdates/2001/110901.htm

15. "Secretary of Labor Chao's Lawsuit Involving Enron Corporation Retirement Plans." US Department of Labor

Factsheet PDF. http://www.dol.gov/_sec/media/announcem ents/factsheet-lawsuit.pdf.

16. Tyco Fraud Infocenter. http://www.tycofraudinfocenter.com/information.php.

17. Tyco International Report TXT file. Securities Exchange Commission, September 10, 2002.
http://www.sec.gov/Archives/edgar/data/833444/000091205702035700/0000912057-02-035700.txt

18. Ussery, Michael J., "Enron: The Implosion.", Accounting Failures.com, January, 2003.
http://www.accountingfailures.com/Enron/enron.htm

19. U.S. GAAP. CPAClass.com, 2004. http://cpaclass.com/gaap/gaap-us-01a.htm

20. Walsh, Anthony F., "The Synthetic Lease: An Introduction and Practice Guide." FindLaw, 1999.
http://library.findlaw.com/1999/Dec/1/131133.html

21. Weinberg, Ari, "The Tyco Follies." Forbes.com, September 18, 2002.
http://www.forbes.com/2002/09/18/0918tyco.html

Whistleblower Policy and Mechanism in India

Dr. T. Sathyanaryana Chary
Tatikonda Neelakantam
M. Swathi

ABSTRACT

'Whistleblowing' is an increasingly common element of regulatory enforcement programs, and one that is encouraged by recent legislation in the US, India and elsewhere. We examine how responsive regulators should be to whistleblower tip-offs, and how severe should penalties be for wrongdoers detected in this way. Competing psychological theories as to what motivates employees to become whistleblowers are operationalized as alternative behavioral heuristics. Optimal policy depends upon the motives attributed to whistleblowers—which of the theories you subscribe to—but is not in general characterized by maximal penalties or routine pursuit of complaints, even when pursuit is costless. This paper focuses on the purpose of whistle blowing policy, legal framework of whistle-blowing policy and whistleblowing policy mechanism in India.

Keywords: Regulation, enforcement, behavioral law and economics. etc.

Introduction

A whistleblower is a person who raises a concern about wrongdoing occurring in an organization or body of people. Usually this person would be from that same organization. The revealed misconduct may be classified in many ways; for example, a violation of a law, rule, regulation and/or a direct threat to public interest, such as fraud, health/safety violations, and corruption. Whistleblowers may make their allegations internally (for example, to other people within the accused organization) or externally (to regulators, law enforcement agencies, to the media or to groups concerned with the issues). Whistleblowers frequently face reprisal, sometimes at the hands of the organization or group which they have accused, sometimes from related organizations, and sometimes under law.

Origins of Term

The term whistleblower derives from the practice of English police officers, who would blow their whistles when they noticed the commission of a crime. The whistle would alert other law enforcement officers and the general public of danger. Most whistleblowers are internal whistleblowers, who report misconduct on a fellow employee or superior within their company. One of the most interesting questions with respect to internal whistleblowers is why and under what circumstances people will either act on the spot to stop illegal and otherwise unacceptable behavior or report it. There is some reason to believe that people are more likely to take action with respect to unacceptable behavior, within an organization, if there are complaint systems that offer not just options dictated by the planning and control organization, but a choice of options for individuals, including an option that offers near absolute confidentiality.

External whistleblowers, however, report misconduct on outside persons or entities. In these cases, depending on the information's severity and nature, whistleblowers may report the misconduct to lawyers, the media, law enforcement or watchdog agencies, or other local, state, or federal agencies. In some cases, external whistleblowing is encouraged by offering monetary reward.

Under most U.S. federal whistleblower statutes, in order to be considered a whistleblower, the federal employee must have reason to believe his or her employer has violated some law, rule or regulation; testify or commence a legal proceeding on the legally protected matter; or refuse to violate the law. In cases where whistleblowing on a specified topic is protected by statute, U.S. courts have generally held that such whistleblowers are protected from retaliation. However, a closely divided U.S. Supreme Court decision, *Garcetti vs. Ceballos* (2006) held that the First Amendment, free speech guarantees for government employees, do not protect disclosures made within the scope of the employees' duties.

Ideas about whistle blowing vary widely. Whistleblowers are commonly seen as selfless martyrs for public interest and organizational accountability; others view them as a 'tattle tale' or "snitches" (slang), solely pursuing personal glory and fame. Some academics (such as Thomas Alured Faunce) consider that whistleblowers should at least be entitled to a rebuttable presumption that they are attempting to apply ethical principles in the face of obstacles and that whistle blowing would be more respected in governance systems if it had a firmer academic basis in virtue ethics. It is probable that many people do not even consider blowing the whistle, not only because of fear of retaliation, but also because of fear of losing their relationships at work and outside work. Because the majority of cases are very low-profile and receive little or no media attention and because whistleblowers who do report significant misconduct are usually put in some form of danger or persecution, the idea of seeking fame and glory may be less commonly believed. Persecution of whistleblowers has become a serious issue in many parts of the world. Although whistleblowers are often protected under law from employer retaliation, there have been many cases where punishment for whistle blowing has occurred, such as termination, suspension, demotion, wage garnishment, and/or harsh mistreatment by other employees. For example, in the United States, most whistleblower protection laws provide for limited "make whole" remedies or damages for employment losses if whistleblower retaliation is proven. However, many whistleblowers report there exists a widespread "shoot the messenger" mentality by corporations or government agencies accused of misconduct and in some cases whistleblowers have been subjected to criminal prosecution in reprisal for reporting wrongdoing.

As a reaction to this many private organizations have formed whistleblower legal defense funds or support groups to assist whistleblowers; one such example in the UK is 'Public Concern at Work'. Depending on the circumstances, it is not uncommon for whistleblowers to be ostracized by their co-workers, discriminated against by future potential employers, or even fired from their organization. This campaign directed at whistleblowers with the goal of eliminating them from the organization is referred to as mobbing. It is an extreme form of workplace bullying wherein the group is set against the targeted individual.

Legal Protection

In the United States, legal protections vary according to the subject matter of the whistleblowing, and sometimes the state in which the case arises. In passing the 2002 Sarbanes-Oxley Act, the Senate Judiciary Committee found that whistleblower protections were dependent on the "patchwork and vagaries" of varying state statutes. Still, a wide variety of federal and state laws protect employees who call attention to violations, help with enforcement proceedings, or refuse to obey unlawful directions. The first U.S. law adopted specifically to protect whistleblowers was the Lloyd-La Follette Act of 1912. It guaranteed the right of federal employees to furnish information to the United States Congress. The first U.S. environmental law to include an employee protection was the Water Pollution Control Act of 1972, also called the Clean Water Act. Similar protections were included in subsequent federal environmental laws including the Safe Drinking Water Act (1974), Resource Conservation and Recovery Act (also called the Solid Waste Disposal Act) (1976), Toxic Substances Control Act (1976), Energy Reorganization Act of 1974 (through 1978 amendment to protect nuclear whistleblowers), Comprehensive Environmental Response, Compensation, and Liability Act (CERCLA, or the Superfund Law) (1980), and the Clean Air Act (1990). Similar employee protections enforced through (Occupational Safety and Health Administration) are included in the Surface Transportation Assistance Act (1982) to protect truck drivers, the Pipeline Safety Improvement Act (PSIA) of 2002, the Wendell H. Ford Aviation Investment and Reform Act for the 21st Century ("AIR 21"), and the Sarbanes-Oxley Act, enacted on July 30, 2002 (for corporate fraud whistleblowers).

The patchwork of laws means that victims of retaliation need to be alert to the laws at issue to determine the deadlines and means for making proper complaints. Some deadiines are as short as 10 days (for Arizona State Employees to file a "Prohibited Personnel Practice" Complaint before the Arizona State Personnel Board; and Ohio public employees to file appeals with the State Personnel Board of Review). It is 30 days for environmental whistleblowers to make a written complaint to the OSHA. Federal employees complaining of discrimination, retaliation or other violations of the civil rights laws have 45 days to make a written complaint to their agency's equal employment opportunity (EEO) officer. Airline workers and corporate fraud whistleblowers have 90 days to make their complaint to OSHA. Nuclear whistleblowers and truck drivers have 180 days to make complaints to OSHA. Victims of retaliation against union organizing and other concerted activities to improve working conditions have six months to make complaints to the National Labor Relations Board (NLRB). Private sector employees have either 180 or 300 days to make complaints to the federal Equal Employment Opportunity Commission (EEOC) (depending on whether their state has a "deferral" agency) for discrimination claims on the basis of race, gender, age, national origin or religion. Those who face retaliation for seeking minimum wages or overtime have either two or three years to file a civil lawsuit, depending on whether the court finds the violation was "willful".

Those who report a false claim against the federal government, and suffer adverse employment actions as a result, may have up to six years (depending on state law) to file a civil suit for remedies under the U.S. False Claims Act (FCA). Under a *qui tam* provision, the "original source" for the report may be entitled to a percentage of what the government recovers from the offenders. However, the "original source" must also be the first to file a federal civil complaint for recovery of the federal funds fraudulently obtained, and must avoid publicizing the claim of fraud until the U.S. Justice Department decides whether to prosecute the claim itself. Such *qui tam* lawsuits must be filed under seal, using special procedures to keep the claim from becoming public until the federal government makes its decision on direct prosecution.

Federal employees could benefit from the Whistleblower Protection Act, and the No FEAR Act (which made individual agencies directly responsible for the economic sanctions of unlawful retaliation). Federal protections are enhanced in those few cases where the Office of Special Counsel will uphold the whistleblower's case.

The Military Whistleblower Protection Act protects the right of members of the armed services to communicate with any member of Congress (even if copies of the communication are sent to others). Legal protection for whistle blowing varies from country to country. In the United Kingdom, the Public Interest Disclosure Act, 1998 provides a framework of legal protection for individuals who disclose information so as to expose malpractice and matters of similar concern. In the vernacular, it protects whistleblowers from victimization and dismissal.

Managing Whistleblowing:

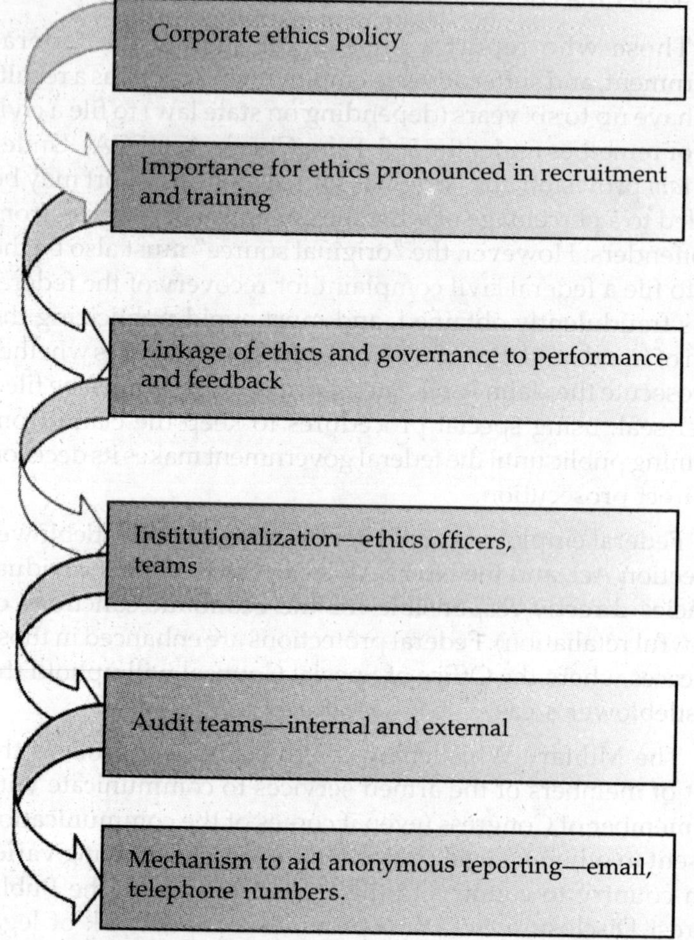

WHISTLEBLOWING MECHANISM IN INDIA

India's whistleblowing mechanisms are "still at a nascent stage" compared to the West, says Arihant Jain of OP Khaitan & Co. "There are also many who believe Western models of laws to protect the whistleblower can't be copied because the Indian situation is unique and beset with challenges," he adds. "Other countries doing business in India believe there is an urgent need to protect whistleblowers," says ML Bhakta, the managing partner of Kanga & Co in Mumbai. India modelled its languishing 2006 whistleblower protection bill (which has yet to be passed into law) on the UK's 1998 Public Interest Disclosure Act. The UK Act allows employees to make "protected disclosures" if they have reasonable grounds to suspect the law has been broken, or that there has been a breach of environmental, health and/or safety regulations. In the US, the Sarbanes-Oxley Act was adopted after the Enron and WorldCom debacles. It requires that publicly traded companies adopt procedures for employees to file internal complaints and maintain confidentiality, and criminalizes retaliation against whistleblowers. "Anyone retaliating against a corporate whistleblower can now be imprisoned for up to 10 years," explain Sukhpreet Singh and Anindita Roy Chowdhury of LexCounsel. Ramya Mohan of Economic Laws Practice laments that "such an exhaustive piece of legislation is absent in India." The US is "generally considered a pioneer in enacting whistleblowing legislation," having done so in relation to the public sector as early as 1989, says Douglas Tween at Baker & McKenzie in New York. "Whistleblowers are generally perceived by the public as heroic figures taking a stand against corrupt authority and bringing corporate or government misdeeds into the light," adds Tween. Not so in India, where whistleblowers "tend to be perceived as acting more in their own selfish interest and less for the collective good." In France there are legal protections for a civil servant who blow the whistle, but not for employees in the private sector, say Jain. He adds that in Germany civil servants may blow the whistle on serious crimes directly to a prosecutor rather to than their immediate supervisor, though no such mechanism exists in the private sector. Across much of Europe there is a widespread feeling that whistleblowing is akin to ratting out friends and colleagues to the secret police, says one American lawyer, adding that strong unions have reinforced that cultural point. "If we're not quite there yet in Europe, we're certainly not there in India," says Suzanne Rab at Hogan & Hartson. Still, India is not exactly lagging behind other Asian countries when it comes to whistleblowing. "The Indian scenario is not very different from that seen in other developing nations, or in Asian economies in general," says Anuj Puri at Jones Lang LaSalle Meghraj. "In these countries, large corporates are often seen as entities whose activities and objectives are at odds with those of the common man. Unless the fraud is extremely large and apparent, the informer is invariably seen as a traitor and is treated accordingly, even if the facts of the case reveal that he or she acted for the greater good." India's laws regarding whistleblowing are ineffectual, narrow in scope, easily eluded or not properly enforced because they merely make recommendations instead of laying down mandatory requirements. Below are a few examples:

Clause 49

This clause (in the listing agreement that is required between a company and a stock exchange at the time of listing) states only that a company may have a whistleblowing policy. It is recommended, but not required. As Singhania & Partners, managing partner Ravi Singhania explains, this "attempt to mandate whistleblower protection has been disregarded by the corporate sector with the argument that it would only empower disgruntled employees to harass the management." SEBI listened to those reservations, and made the requirement non-mandatory.

Whistleblowers (Protection in Public Interest Disclosures) Bill

This bill was introduced in India's parliament in March 2006. The bill purportedly "provides for protection from criminal or civil liability, departmental inquiry, demotion, harassment and discrimination of whistleblowers", says Arihant Jain of OP Khaitan & Co. The bill is still pending in parliament. Even if it does make it through, many lawyers are sceptical. Arti Narsana and Ann Jose of Vaish Associates call the bill "a rudimentary form" of the UK Public Interest Disclosure Act. "The bill is very sketchy and does not set up a definite mechanism for protection of whistleblowers," says ML Bhakta, managing partner of Kanga & Co.

Central Vigilance Commission (CVC)

Ramya Mohan, a partner at Economic Laws Practice, says that after Satyendra Dubey's murder, the government passed a resolution authorizing the CVC to receive written complaints on allegations of corruption or the misuse of office, and to recommend appropriate action in response. However, Mohan says, this order only covers employees of the central government, or of companies and authorities owned or controlled by the government: "It does not cover employees of private sector organizations," he says. "The practicality is that the CVC has done little and the common man lacks any faith in any enforcement by it," adds Pooja Yadava of PSA Legal Counsellors in New Delhi.

Reserve Bank of India (RBI) Rules

In 2007 the RBI adopted a resolution similar to that governing the CVC, this time applying to private and foreign banks. "However," says Mohan, "the role of the RBI in this regard is again recommendatory [only]." As Debjani Aich-Ramnath of Kochhar & Co notes, "Unfortunately, there is no similar specific legal protection available to whistleblower employees in the corporate sector in India."

Conclusion

Some key concepts to incorporate in a good whistleblower protection policy include:

Anonymity & confidentiality: Your policy should provide a way for people to express complaints anonymously, while pointing out that anonymity can hinder an investigation of the complaint. Otherwise, the policy should promise confidentiality to the extent possible.

Good faith: Be clear in explaining that the policy is based on people acting in good faith to report concerns that they have reason to believe are true, while noting that the organization could take disciplinary action against anyone who makes unfounded allegations that are proven to have been made recklessly, maliciously or with the foreknowledge that the allegations were false.

No retaliation: The policy should assure employees that your organization has a zero-tolerance policy for retaliation, and that any employee who reports possible violations in good faith will not experience abuse, harassment, threats, discrimination or any adverse employment consequences as a result. The policy can also state the possible consequences for anyone who retaliates against an individual who reports a suspected violation.

References

1. Winters v. Houston Chronicle Pub. Co., 795 S.W.2d 723, 727 (Tex. 1990) (Doggett, J., concurring).
2. Mary Rowe, "Options and Choice for Conflict Resolution in the Workplace" in *Negotiation: Strategies for Mutual Gain*, by Lavinia Hall, ed., Sage Publications, Inc., 1993, pp. 105–119.
3. Faunce, TA, "Developing and Teaching the Virtue-Ethics" *Foundations of Healthcare Whistleblowing Monash Bioethics Review* 2004; 23(4): 41-55.
4. Faunce, TA and Jefferys, S., "Whistleblowing and Scientific Misconduct: Renewing Legal and Virtue Ethics Foundations", *Journal of Medicine and Law* 2007, 26 (3): 567-84.
5. *Congressional Record*, p. S7412; S. Rep. No. 107-146, 107th Cong., 2d Session 19 (2002).
6. Quentin Dempster, *Whistleblowers*, Sydney, ABC Books, 1997. ISBN 0-7333-0504-0 [See especially pp. 199–212: 'The Courage of the Whistleblowers']
7. Frais, A, "Whistleblowing heroes—boon or burden"? *Bulletin of Medical Ethics*, 2001 Aug. (170): 13-19.
8. Alford, C. Fred (2001), *Whistleblowers: Broken Lives and Organizational Power*, Cornell University Press. ISBN 0-8014-3841-1.
9. Garrett, Allison, "Auditor Whistleblowing: The Financial Fraud Detection and Disclosure Act," 17 Seton Hall Legis. J. 91 (1993).
10. Hesch, Joel (2009), *Whistleblowing: A guide to government reward programs,* Goshen Press. ISBN 978-0977260201.
11. Hunt, Geoffrey (2000), "Whistleblowing, Accountability & Ethical Accounting", in *Clinical Risk* 6(3): 115-16.
12. Hunt, Geoffrey (1998), *'Whistleblowing', commissioned entry for Encyclopedia of Applied Ethics,* (8,000 words), Academic Press, California, USA.

13. Hunt, Geoffrey (ed) (1998), *Whistleblowing in the Social Services: Public Accountability & Professional Practice,* Arnold.

14. Hunt, G (ed) (1995), *Whistleblowing in the Health Service: Accountability, Law & Professional Practice,* Arnold.

15. Johnson, Roberta Ann (2002), *Whistleblowing: When It Works—And Why,* L. Reinner Publishers. ISBN 978-1588261144.

16. Kohn, Stephen M., (2000), *Concepts and Procedures in Whistleblower Law,* Quorum Books. ISBN 1-56720-354-X.

17. Kohn, Stephen M; Kohn, Michael D; Colapinto, David K. (2004), *Whistleblower Law, A Guide to Legal Protections for Corporate Employees,* Praeger Publishers. ISBN 0-275-98127 4.

18. Lauretano, Major Daniel A., "The Military Whistleblower Protection Act and the Military Mental Health Protection Act", *Army Law,* (Oct) 1998.

19. Miethe, Terance D (1991), *Whistleblowing at work: tough choices in exposing fraud, waste, and abuse on the job,* Westview Press. ISBN 0-81—33-3549-3.

20. "Sarbanes-Oxley Criminal Whistleblower Provisions & the Workplace: More Than Just Securities Fraud," by Jay P. Lechner & Paul M. Sisco, 80 Florida B. J. 85 (June 2006).

Evolution of Corporate Social Responsibility

Its use for business purpose

Prof. Syed Jaffer

ABSTRACT

Corporate social responsibility (CSR) is an evolving concept. In the business community CSR is alternatively referred to as "corporate citizenship", which essentially means that a company should be a "good neighbour", within its host community. With the given understanding that business have a key role of job and wealth creation in a society, corporate social responsibility (CSR) is generally understood to be the way an organization achieves a balance between economic, environmental, and social imperatives while they address the expectations of the shareholders and stakeholders.

Today more and more companies are realizing that in order to stay productive, competitive and relevant in a rapidly changing business world, they have to become socially responsible. India is a fast growing economy and is booming with national and multinational firms. At the same time, the Indian land also faces social challenges like poverty, population growth, corruption, illiteracy etc.

CSR is a good 'business case'. Companies invest in CSR activities because it makes business sense. It is neither a pure philanthropic activity which aims to 'do good to the community' nor an activity that aims to 'pay back to the society'.

Companies align CSR projects with business strategy. Therefore, companies select those projects which support the company's business strategy directly or indirectly. Companies often select projects which will augment the market for inputs or outputs. Companies should select projects that are of national importance or which are important to the local community. They should involve employees in selecting the project. This practice enhances employee satisfaction. This will benefit the society as well as the employee a sense of satisfaction towards doing something to the society.

Introduction

Corporate social responsibility (CSR) is an evolving concept. In the business community CSR is alternatively referred to as "corporate citizenship", which essentially means that a company should be a "good neighbour", within its host community. With the given understanding that business have a key role of job and wealth creation in a society, corporate social responsibility (CSR) is generally understood to be the way an organization achieves a balance between economic, environmental, and social imperatives while they address the expectations of the shareholders and stakeholders. CSR takes into account and helps the business to create and maintain effective with the stakeholders. It means taking a responsible attitude, going beyond the minimum requirements and following straight forward principles that apply, whatever the size of your business. Corporate social responsibility is a function of operating a business that meets or exceeds the ethical, legal, commercial and public expectations that society has of business.

A simple definition of CSR might be adhering to the laws and regulations while a value-laden definition of CSR could be doing business with high regard to morality.

The concept of CSR can be understood in the form of 'triple bottom line' approach, that explained that for an organization to be sustainable, it should be financially secure, it must minimize or ideally eliminate the environmental impacts and most important is that it must act in conformity with societal expectations.

CSR focuses on the following six points: Improving business performance and strengthening sustainability of corporate development under the conditions of legal and trust-oriented management and maintenance of a sound market economy order; protecting legal rights of the employees; building a harmonious and stable working relationship; consolidating work safety and guaranteeing employees' safety and health. Apart from these we also need to make efforts in public welfare participation and environmental protection by reducing consumption of resources in order to speed up the construction of a harmonious society.

Today more and more companies are realizing that in order to stay productive, competitive and relevant in a rapidly changing business world, they have to become socially responsible. In the last two decades, globalization has blurred national borders and technology accelerated time and masked distance. Given this change in the corporate environment, companies want to increase their ability to manage their profits and risks to protect the reputation of their brands. While CSR is relevant for business in all societies, it is particularly significant for developing countries like India, where limited resources for meeting the ever growing aspirations and diversity of a pluralistic society, make process of sustainable development more challenging.

CSR and Historical Developments

Corporate social responsibility has its roots in the thinking of the twentieth century where the theologians and the religious thinkers suggested the application of religious principles to business activities. Religious charity and giving exists across the country,and the world from the time immemorial. The Sikh community who donate "dasvandh" (one tenth) to society, feed the poor and perform charitable action. The Muslims also donate a part of their income to the needy and poor in the form of Zakat and Fitra for the upliftment of the poor.

Post-independence India saw the growth of the public sector, many of whom had a "community development focus". The Tata's, through their various trusts in early nineteenth century, showed the way to the rest of the world in terms of working hours and social security measures, earning them goodwill for many future decades. However, corporate responsibility was rarely practiced by senior management teams in a strategic way across sectors. Post-1990, India adopted a policy of liberalization and many Multi- and Trans- National Corporations (MNCs/TNCs) made forays into the growing Indian market. Very few foreign companies had a robust CSR programme nor were they known for responsible practices, in fact the practice of double standards was rampant where companies took advantage of weak regularity environments to get away with shoddy goods and weak consumer services. But, now more and more Indian companies have started benchmarking global business procedures in the post-liberalization period.

Emerging Markets: Evolution of CSR in Developing Economies

Corporate social responsibility is a term describing a company's obligation to be accountable to all of its stakeholders in all its operations and activities. Socially responsible companies consider the full scope of their impact on communities and the environment when making decisions, balancing the needs of stakeholders with their need to make a profit. A company's stakeholders are all those who are influenced by and can influence a company's decisions and actions, both locally and globally.

India is a fast growing economy and is booming with national and multinational firms. At the same time, the Indian land also faces social challenges like poverty, population growth, corruption, illiteracy etc. Therefore, it is all the more imperative for the Indian companies to be sensitivized to CSR in the right perspective in order to facilitate and create an enabling environment for equitable partnership between the civil society and business. CSR provides the benefits to the organization to gain goodwill in society.

The evolution of CSR in the developing economies shows widely varying results:

Chambers, Chapple, Moon and Sullivan (2003) evaluate the extent of CSR penetration in seven Asian countries (India, Indonesia, Malaysia, the Philippines, Singapore, South Korea and Thailand), and show that the mean value for the seven countries (even including industrially advanced Japan) is just 41 per cent compared to say a score of 98 per cent for a developed nation like the United Kingdom.

However, there are exceptions to the mean scores. India, for example, had an average CSR penetration of 72 per cent compared to Indonesia's 24 per cent. The concept of CSR as visualized in the emerging markets and the developed countries have very different understanding.

Defining Corporate Social Responsibility

Theodore Levitt (1958) could be credited with setting the agenda for the debate about the social responsibility of business in his *Harvard Business Review* article 'The Dangers of Social Responsibility', in which he cautions that 'government's job is not business, and business's job is not government'.

Milton Friedman (1970) expressed the same sentiment and added that the mere existence of CSR was a signal of an agency problem within the firm. An agency theory perspective implies that CSR is a misuse of corporate resources that would be better spent on valued-added internal projects or returned to shareholders. It also suggests that CSR is an executive perk, in the sense that managers use CSR to advance their careers or other personal agendas.

Donaldson and Davis (1991): Another perspective, stewardship theory is based on the idea that there is a moral imperative for managers to 'do the right thing', without regard to how such decisions affect the firm's financial performance.

Donaldson and Preston (1995) who stressed the moral and ethical dimensions of CSR, as well as the business case for engaging in such activity.

Russo and Fouts (1997) tested this theory empirically using firm-level data on environmental and accounting profitability and found that firms with higher levels of environmental performance had superior financial performance, which they interpreted to be consistent with the RBV theory.

McWilliams et al. (2002) applied the RBV framework to demonstrate how US firms can use political strategies, based on CSR, to raise regulatory barriers that prevent foreign competitors from using substitute (e.g. low labour cost) technology.

Corporate Social responsibility is best defined by the World Business Council (2006) as "The continuing commitment by business to behave ethically and contribute to economic development while improving the quality of life of the workforce and their families as well as of the local community and society at large".

Need for CSR

CSR is about how companies manage the business processes to produce an overall positive impact on society.

The World Business Council for Sustainable Development in its publication "Making Good Business Sense" by Lord Holme and Richard Watts, used the following definition. "Corporate Social Responsibility is the continuing commitment by business to behave ethically and contribute to economic development while improving the quality of life of the workforce and their families as well as of the local community and society at large".

According to ICAI secretary Ashok Haldia in his correspondence with *Times of India*, one of the leading newspapers in India, "It is to ensure that today's development and growth does not come at the cost of the future generation".

The Role of Business Ethics and Corporate Social Responsibility in Business Management

Business ethics and CSR go hand in hand. In order to understand CSR, one must also understand ethics. Also, a socially responsible firm should also be an ethical firm and an ethical firm should also be a socially responsible firm. Researchers are making it increasingly clear that the two concepts are essential for long-term sustainability of an organisation. In today's highly competitive business environment, business ethics and CSR are no more an option but a necessary practice activity for all organisations. Therefore, business ethics and CSR continue to be important to organisations and strong ethical value shall take an organisation a long way forward.

CSR: An Expenditure or Asset

JJ Irani, Director, Tata Sons at annual conclave, organized by the Indian Institute of Management, Lucknow (IIM-L) said that "the corporate social responsibility (CSR) is the future investment for any company and it is not only about giving back to the community but also fostering an environment of strong corporate governance".

Benefits of CSR

Companies have been encouraged to adopt and expand CSR efforts as a result of pressures from customers, employees, communities, investors, activist organizations and other stake holders. As a result CSR has grown dramatically in recent years (Centre for Corporate Research and Training, 2003). Companies have experienced a range of bottom line benefits from being engaged in CSR which include.

- Enhanced corporate image and added brand value
- Customer satisfaction and loyalty
- Access to quality business partners
- Favourable access to capital markets
- Established a good footing with public authorities and the general public
- Public relations opportunities
- Improved financial performance
- Increased productivity, sales and quality
- Increased ability to attract and retain employees

- Gained confidence of customers, suppliers, employees, communities, investors, activist organizations and other stakeholders.

CSR in India

In the Indian context, CSR is not a new concept. Businessmen were treated with great respect because of prevalence of the concept of parting with one's wealth for the benefit of the society. Merchants have always been charitable and provided relief in difficult times like droughts, famine or epidemics. Over the years this practice remained same except shift from merchant charity to corporate citizenship. Indian companies are groping in different directions. Caught in cancer hospitals, schools and colleges, vocational schools, scholarships , carbon footprints, adoption of villages to provide basic amenities, or launching a public communication campaigns, creating income generating schemes and community development work are some of the initiatives taken by the corporates.

There are some companies that have taken CSR to be making up or undoing the harm to the ecosystem from their pollution-spewing factories or mining of the earth.

"Though most of the Indian companies want to be socially responsible, hardly any understand what that entails," says professor at JN University of Social Sciences, Dipankar Gupta. Few such as ITC, are going about their corporate social responsibility (CSR) the way they ought to. They are doing right by mainstreaming social responsibility in to every business decision, even extending it to supply chains. Doing good, to them, is the way of earning, not spending.

India has 37.2 per cent of its population as per the Planning Commission living below the poverty line, an agrarian and water crisis, income disparities and lack of access to basic necessities, therefore as country it requires calls for action from all stakeholders including the corporate sector which can respond with not just financial resources but also with strategies, tools & management techniques that can address development priorities in the country.

Unfortunately, the track record of corporate India has been less than exemplary when it comes to CSR of any sort. Whatever efforts are taken up, are welcome and laudable. But they are not enough to make a visible impact on India. Further, a potentially disturbing development may also be in the making. With global warming and environmental degradation occupying (rightfully) much international and national attention, many large businesses have (again, rightfully) also focused their attention on "sustainability". The risk is that environmentally responsible business practices are now actually a business imperative, and should not be seen as CSR per se.

With many Indian (and international) companies now reaching billion or multi-billion dollar revenue scale in India, they should consider deploying some of their formidable innovation, product development, manufacturing, distributing, marketing, and managerial skills towards coming out with truly revolutionary, paradigm-altering products and services providing appropriate, cost-effective solutions to those hundreds of millions of Indians at the bottom of the pyramid. Merely allocating a few crores of rupees or a couple of million dollars for product R&D—either in-house or through third parties and NGOs—will, sadly, not be enough. Stripped down versions of existing products and services in an attempt to make them more affordable to the masses may also not really be enough.

India's challenges, while humungous, are easy to identify and understand. Hundreds of millions are deprived of basic physical and social infrastructure, which includes potable water, basic sanitation and hand-wash solutions, clean energy for lighting and cooking, basic housing, dietary supplements to make good deficiency in critical minerals and vitamins, primary health care, affordable personal transportation and elementary education that includes imparting of a basic understanding of their political and civic rights and obligations. In this backdrop, truly laudable and potentially very high impact CSR effort could be when giants such as Reliance, Tata,

Birla, HUL, P&G, Nirma, Bharti, Essar, Mittal Arcelor, Godrej, Apollo, Max, Fortis, GE, Philips, LG, Samsung, Videocon, Maruti, Hyundai, Mahindra, Manipal, Amity, Raymond, Arvind, DLF, GMR, GVK, Infosys, Wipro, Bennett Coleman, Dainik Bhaskar, IBM, HP, HCL and others take up the challenge of finding revolutionary out-of-the-box solutions to these challenges. Each of these giants do have the capability to line up intellectual and financial resources from across the planet to come up with out-of-the-box approaches and path-breaking technologies that can help India (and indeed, the poor across the world) provide some succour and hope to its deprived and needy.

As in the case of developing products and solutions for the well-off, the starting point has to be the end "customer". The approach has to be "customer" and "context" centric. If at all a fortune has to be sought from serving those at the bottom of the pyramid, it must be measured in their smiles and happiness, and return on capital to be monitored through the success achieved in tackling of the challenge. Would the shareholders of such large public and private enterprises allow such investments? There is enough reason to believe that they would give their assent provided these are reasonable in the context of the size of such enterprises and have a well-articulated vision and action plan championed by owner-promoters or the CEOs themselves.

Business Case

CSR is a good 'business case'. Companies invest in CSR activities because it makes business sense. It is neither a pure philanthropic activity which aims to 'do good to the community' nor an activity that aims to 'pay back to the society'.

Companies invest in CSR activities because they derive significant benefits from those activities. CSR activities help companies to build reputation, make environment less vindictive, reduce litigation, and attract talent. In addition to those benefits, companies that invest in CSR activities develop good understanding of social culture and dynamics and identify social changes much in advance of those companies which are not involved in CSR activities. Visionary companies identify social undercurrents and latent social needs and often convert them in business opportunities. CSR is a very potent tool for managing reputational risks.

It is unfortunate that many companies try to present CSR activities as purely philanthropic. This might be a public posture, but this set a wrong tone in the organisation and employees fail to see the 'business case' and act with the perception that CSR activities are discretionary in nature. This is detrimental to the long term interest of the company.

CSR more Strategic than Tactical Tool

Corporate Social Responsibility (CSR) is now playing a strategic role than a tactical role that it used to earlier. Some 15 years ago, firms could take up CSR works as a means to save taxes; firms today have to take up CSR work as an integral part of the firm's operations if they need to succeed in the global market. This often gives firms an edge in the market and helps them find business partners from many parts of the world to work with.

According to Vasanthi Srinivasan, associate professor, IIM-B, "Firms today can end up losing a lot if they do not have credible CSR programmes. Also, the kind of CSR work a firm takes up matters and can dictate how easy it will be for them to do business or find business partners.

Selection of CSR Projects

Companies align CSR projects with business strategy. Therefore, companies select those projects which support the company's business strategy directly or indirectly. Companies often select projects which will augment the market for inputs or outputs. For example, a steel company may develop villages surrounding its plant for the welfare of its employees and to ensure that future employees, who are inhabitants of the village, will be healthy and educated. Similarly, a company engaged in software business invests in spreading computer education to create markets for inputs (e.g. skilled employees) and output (e.g. software). In selecting projects companies also consider the level of satisfaction that employees will derive from each project.

Conclusion

CSR initiatives make good 'business case' and therefore there is no need to provide fiscal incentives from tax payers' money. It is also incorrect to expect that CSR initiatives will benefit the most deserving groups (e.g. weaker sections) in the society. They cannot replace government initiatives for social development.

The majority of the "corporates in India are moving from philanthropy to project-based CSR." They are yet to understand that what they are doing—more commendable than not doing at all, as it may be—is not CSR. The vast majority of the Indian sector is writing cheques to NGOs or charitable institutions, whatever the work has been done, it is better to take up work that will benefit the society.

With increasing and widespread commitment of corporate resources to CSR, attention is now shifting to the strategic formulation, implementation, and measurement of the market returns to CSR initiatives. But still a concern to companies is whether their focus on "doing good," will provide positive returns to their CSR actions.

Companies should select projects that are of national importance or which are important to the local community. They should involve employees in selecting the project. This practice enhances employee satisfaction. Companies should collaborate with voluntary organisations to implement CSR projects in order to improve the quality of delivery and achieve economy of scale. It is observed that often companies selects similar projects in the same region and compete with each other. This results in waste of resources. It may be good idea that companies pool their resources to maximize benefits to target beneficiaries.

The research report issued by the Times Foundation reports that most CSR activities are carried out in urban areas and covers people near the organisation or industry. Therefore, rural poor are largely untouched by corporate CSR initiatives. Companies do not necessarily target projects to weaker sections of the society because their objective is to maximise benefits from those initiatives.

References

1. Hakhu Rahul, "Corporate Social Responsibility—An Indian Perspective", *Advances in Management*, Vol. 3(6), June 2010.
2. H. S. Sandhu and Shveta Kapoor, "Corporate Social Responsibility Initiatives: An analysis of voluntary corporate disclosure", *South Asian Journal of Management*, Vol. 17, Issue No. 2, April-June 2010.
3. Harsh Vineet Kaur & Gurvinder Kaur, "Facets of Corporate Social Responsibility in today's era-A case study of Mahindra And Mahindra Ltd", *Prabandhan: Indian Journal of Management*, Vol. 3, Number 7, July, 2010.
4. Dr. M. K. Ramakrishnan, Reshma K. P., "Corporate Social Responsibility Initiatives of companies in India", *Prabandhan: Indian Journal of Management*, Vol. 3, Number 7, July, 2010.
5. *Businessworld*, 26 May 2008.
6. *Advanced Strategic Management*, (Course Number Ms-91), IGNOU Study Material.
7. www.iitk.ac.in/infocell/announce/convention/papers/Industrial Economics, Environment, CSR-07-VijayLaxmi Iyengar.pdf(1).
8. Dr. Sanjeev Verma & Rohit Chauhan, "Role of Corporate Social Responsibility in Developing Economies", International Marketing Conference on Marketing & Society, 8-10 April, 2007, IIMK.

Websites

http://business.outlookindia.com/wirenews_new.aspx?newsid=23686 & source=bw

www.itcportal.com/sets/echoupal_frameset.htm

www.csr-asia.com/

www.karmayog.org/

www.csr360gpn.org/magazine/feature/a-picture-of-csr-in-india/

www.oppapers.com/essays/The-Role-Of-Business-Ethics-And/302611?read_essay(2)

www.business-standard.com

www.emeraldresearch.com-SSRN-id754564.

Ownership Patterns and Effectiveness of Clause 49

To instill corporate governance in the indian corporate

Prof. Shanti Suresh
Prof. Siva Kumar SNV

ABSTRACT

Clause 49 mandates the corporate governance norms to be followed by corporate India. This has been like other legislations borrowed from the United States—a replica of the Sarbanes Oxley Act, 2002. Sarbanes Oxley Act that was a legislation initiated by the US parliament post-Enron, to regulate and monitor the activities of the listed corporate, and ensures that the interests of the owners are protected against the corporate misfeasance by professional managers.

India followed suit with the initiative taken by Confederation of Indian Industry (CII) and subsequently taken over by SEBI, the responsibility to enact a legislation which mandates compliance with stipulated norms of corporate governance inducing transparency and disclosure in all the financial transactions undertaken by the listed corporate.

This paper makes an attempt to study the ownership patterns prevalent in the Indian corporate environment, and tries to validate the impact of the listing agreement norms in protecting the interests of the minority, and preventing corporate misfeasance. Five sectors have been identified that play a pivotal role in the Indian Business, and the ownership patterns are evaluated to identify the degree of effectiveness of Clause 49.

Introduction

Starting with the Constitution, to the entire legislative framework, India, has been adapting, and adopting laws from the western countries mainly UK, and US. India a common law country like many developed nations, follows the Anglo-Saxon Model for instituting a governance mechanism. The designing of the legislative framework for incorporating governance norms is on lines with the Sarbanes Oxley Act, 2002, passed by the United States parliament following the wide corporate collapses like Enron and the like. The stringency of the Sarbanes Oxley Act has not been so well-appreciated by the Corporate community, but the impact has been far reaching in the United States, though questions are again arising as to why the global crisis could not have been averted if corporate were so well- monitored to function in the interest of the stakeholders.

The objectives of this paper are to:

1. study the Indian corporate ownership pattern.
2. evaluate the suitability of the outsider governance model/Anglo- Saxon Model prevalent and practiced in the United States for India.
3. validate the effectiveness of the regulatory standards in ensuring good governance and monitoring the corporate.

The paper is divided into three sections, each of which makes a study of the singular aspects so as to arrive at a consensus, and provide clarity of thoughts.

Section one provides an overview of corporate governance systems and prevalent models across countries, their characteristics and suitability based on the business environment.

Section two evaluates the major requirements in terms of compliance of the Clause 49 of the listing agreement and its suitability to the Indian Corporate environment.

Section three provides an analysis of the Indian Ownership patterns across five sectors, and evaluates the major requisitions in terms of compliance of the Clause 49 of the listing agreement and its suitability to the Indian Corporate environment.

Section I

AN OVERVIEW OF CORPORATE GOVERNANCE SYSTEMS

The Corporate Governance challenge primarily arises out of the separation of ownership and management, and the resultant agency problems. To compound the problem further, the ability of owners to write effective contracts that minimize the problems is getting tougher by the day. Countries across the world, along with the academic community, are researching and reinventing mechanisms and all have started assessing the corporate governance at country or company level, drawing up guidelines and codes of practice to strengthen the governance norms that can effectively reduce agency costs, and overcome the problems of expropriation by unscrupulous directors. International bodies like the World Bank and OECD have developed international guidelines and principles that have been recommended to member nations.

Corporate governance mechanisms differ across countries. The governance mechanism of each country gets shaped by its political, economic and legal history. OECD has taken an effective lead in evolving a set of principles of corporate governance, which are internationally recognized and serve as useful benchmarks. There have also been some welcome initiatives by the stock exchanges across many countries prescribing good governance practices for their listed companies in their countries. Institutional Investors worldwide give a lot of importance to the firms and economies that have a strong legal system, investor protection regulations, and regulations that mandate transparent and globally acceptable accounting and governance standards. Companies that embrace high disclosure and governance standards invariably command better premium in the market and are thus able to raise capital at lower cost.

An optimal corporate governance structure is the one that would minimize institutional costs resulting from the clash of diverging interests between the management and the stakeholders. Over the years individual economies have developed different capital market mechanisms, legal structures, factor markets and private or public institutions to act as owners of corporate governance in the economy.

There are different models of Corporate Governance prevalent around the world. These differ according to the variety of capitalism in which they are embedded. The liberal model that is common in Anglo- American countries tends to give priority to the interest of the shareholders.

The co-ordinate model that one finds in continental Europe and Japan recognizes the interest of workers, managers, suppliers, customers and the community. Both models have distinct competitive advantages. The liberal model of Corporate Governance encourages radical innovation and quality competition. In the US the Corporation is governed by Board of Directors, which has the power to choose Executive Officers known as the CEO. The CEO has broad powers to manage the Corporation on a daily basis, but needs to get Board's approval for certain major decision such as hiring people, raising money, acquiring another company, major capital expansion or other expensive project. Other duties of the board may include policy setting, decision-making monitoring management's performance or corporate control.

Anglo-Saxon countries have a low concentration of shareholders. In the United States and the United Kingdom most of the shares are in the hands of the agents of financial institutions (more than 50%) rather than private persons (20-30%). Due to regulations in the Anglo-Saxon countries, many financial institutions are not allowed to hold shares in publicly listed companies on their own behalf. They mainly act as agents. The shareholdings of financial institutions can be divided into two groups—banks on the one hand, and insurance companies, along with investment and pension funds on the other. Banks hold few shares in the equity of the companies because of conflicts of interest, which appear when they also grant debt to those companies. The Anglo-Saxon Model of corporate governance requires listed companies to have unitary boards, independent outside directors, and board committees. The principles focused on enhancing shareholder value, and in the process richly reward top executives. In this Model shareholders are widely dispersed, in markets that are liquid, with the discipline of hostile bids. Because of the low concentration of shareholders in Anglo-Saxon countries, most shareholders do not have significant power in any firm. This leaves management with the power to decide on many of the problems concerning the company. In the Anglo-Saxon Model, management has the power to make decisions, and these decisions will frequently be in their own interest, which gives rise to over-investment. Management prefers to undertake expansion activities that facilitate the diversification and reduction of their individual risk profile, as this enhances their power. Investments will thus be made even if the profitability is low or negative. Over-investment will thus give power to management, but leaves shareholders with a lower profitability because managers will invest even though profit prospects are poor (Jensen, 1986). Renne Boog (1996) says that if voting power is dispersed, as in Anglo-Saxon countries, free riding will occur. This means that a single shareholder will bear the costs of control, but will only benefit from it in the percentage of his stake in the firm. Because the costs of control exceed the benefits, shareholders tend not to take action. Consequently, management will have dominant power in the firm. This characteristic of the corporate governance system in Anglo-Saxon countries, delegating great power to management, tends to produce a short-term orientation of management.

In the United States, Sarbanes Oxley mandated conformance with corporate governance by law. Whilst in the United Kingdom and those other jurisdictions whose company law has been influenced over the years by UK Common Law, including Australia, Hong Kong, India, Singapore and South Africa, compliance is based on a voluntary 'comply or explain' philosophy. Companies report compliance with the corporate governance code or explain why they have not. The suitability of the Anglo-Saxon system and its competitiveness to regulate and monitor the corporate has become highly questionable after the global crisis.

In Japan, Keiretsu organizational networks spread power around a group of inter-connected companies in ways that might provide insights for complex western groups. The view that business involves relationships with all those involved—employees, customers, suppliers, and society, as well as shareholders, has only recently been recognized in the west under the umbrella of 'corporate social responsibility'.

The governance of Chinese family businesses throughout Eastasia can provide some valuable insights: for example, the emphasis on top-level leadership, the view that the independence of outside directors is less important than their character and business ability, and the way that the Chinese family business sees business more as a succession of trades rather than the building of empires. In China, the link between state, at the national, provincial and local levels, and companies relies on a network of relationships, and policies can be pursued in the interests of the people.

These diverse models reflect more concentrated ownership, different cultures, and varied company law jurisdictions. But they also show different perceptions about the way power should be exercised over corporate entities. In other words people and the way they behave are more important than board structures and strictures, rules and regulations.

Continental European companies hold large stakes in other (related) companies and shareholding also moves in the opposite direction. The existence of different holding and pyramidal structures in these companies regulates the diverse patterns of control, which are often maintained over the long term. Due to the number of mutual shareholdings and the limited extent of information disclosure, the ownership structure in Continental European countries is not as transparent as in Anglo-Saxon countries. Regulations such as anti-trust laws and the "arm's length rule" between parent and daughter companies have limited the complexity of the ownership structure in Anglo-Saxon countries (Van Hulle, 1997).

Because the Continental European model grants great power to a few shareholders, those shareholders will retain control over the firm and make decisions that enhance the profitability of the firm instead of enlarging the firm's size through large investments. They normally invest for a longer time span and thus will be more long-term oriented than managers in the Anglo-Saxon model. In the concentrated shareholder model of Continental Europe, the ownership structure of many firms is characterized by the participation of control and holding structures. Through these mechanisms, shareholders retain power over their investments, while the complex patterns of control deny transparency to the company's structure. Another disadvantage of the Continental European model lies in the limited financial resources that are available to companies. Because ownership is concentrated, only a few owners are suppliers of the equity to the firm. The transfer of cash flow from one company to another is a common practice in Continental European countries. Due to the lack of transparency, companies are able to transfer cash flow from a well performing company to a related, but badly performing company.

The Indian Model

The Indian Model is an amalgam of the Anglo American and German models. The Indian corporate can be typified into two distinct patterns i.e. private companies, public enterprises and the pattern of private companies is, mostly that of closely held or dominated by a promoter group. The role of external equity finance remained low; in the early '80s the business was financed by retained earnings and heavily by debt, like the Tata, Birla and Reliance group. However, since the process of liberalization and globalization there has been a shift in the financing patterns, and equity stakes have assumed high proportion, and the governance issue is that of protecting the interests of the diversified minority shareholders from the vested interests of the dominant shareholder. Agency problems occupy top slot in these concerns. The organizations are run with the prime objective of maximizing profits, and optimizing the interests of the promoter shareholders.

In respect of public enterprises, the primary owners of the business, the majority stakes are held by the central and state governments. In these organizations the protections of the interests of the stakeholders take a back seat. Large corporations are, therefore, often run in the interests of the government and bureaucracy. The objectives are socially driven, which are attained at the cost of profitability and efficiency. The appropriation of corporate opportunities, excessive compensation, and consumption of managerial perks are not relevant as the boards are appointed by the government, and they have to function as per the external policy of the government.

The main characteristic of the Indian Model is the Agency issue primarily is between the dominant promoters who control the management and control of the organization *vs.* the minority shareholders in the organization. Being diffused over a wide geographical region and lack of any shareholder activism in the Indian business environment has made the minority a vulnerable group that has no representation or proxy who could effectively protect their interest against the erring dominant promoters.

Section II

REGULATORY STANDARDS IN ENSURING GOOD GOVERNANCE AND MONITORING THE CORPORATE

Some of the mandatory requirements as prescribed by the Clause 49 are as follows:

1. The requirement of 50 per cent of Independent Directors on the boards of companies which have the Chairman of the board also heading the Management.

2. The appointment of Independent Directors.
3. The appointment of Auditors of the company.
4. The definition of the Independent Directors.
5. Listed companies must have audit committees of the board with a minimum of three directors, two-thirds of whom must be independent, the roles and responsibilities of the audit committee are specified in detail.
6. Listed companies must periodically make various disclosures regarding financial and other matters to ensure transparency.
7. The CEO and CFO of listed companies must:
   i. certify that the financial statements are fair,
   ii. accept responsibility for internal controls, and
   iii. Annual reports of listed companies must carry status reports about compliance with corporate governance norms.

Section III

OWNERSHIP STRUCTURE IN THE INDIAN *CORPORATE ENVIRONMENT*

Dominant shareholders *vs.* the minority shareholders is the crux of all governance problems in the Indian corporate environment. Essentially, there are three large ownership categories in India. First are the public sector units (PSUs), where the government is the dominant/majority shareholder and the general public holds a minority stake, often as little as 20 per cent. Second are the multi-national companies (MNCs), where the foreign parent is the dominant shareholder. Third are the Indian business groups, where the promoters (together with their friends and relatives) are the dominant shareholders with large ownership stakes, the government-owned financial institutions hold a comparable stake, and the balance is held by the general public.

Most Indian companies today are a hybrid of family-owned and publicly listed companies, where most often ownership and management are not diverse. For example, of out of 50 of India's largest public companies on its Nifty Index, only two have a dispersed ownership structure, according to 2007 research by CRISIL. Deutsche Bank research shows that 54 per cent of large Indian companies are controlled by a single family, 16 are majority-owned by foreign investors, and 20 per cent are controlled by the state. In most cases, this control is maintained with as little as 12 per cent to 20 per cent of the voting shares, which, in theory, should make it possible to have a market for corporate control. The governance problems posed by the dominant shareholders in each of the above three categories of companies are different, and governance troubles connected to the predominant form of family ownership has often been that of unprofessional management to direct abuse of minority shareholder rights via related party transactions.

In Indian business groups, the concept of dominant shareholders is more amorphous for two reasons. First, the promoters' shareholding is spread across several friends and relatives as well as corporate entities, which many a times makes it difficult to establish the total effective holding of this group. The actual ownership within these companies is far from being completely transparent with widespread pyramiding, crossholding, and the use of non-public trusts and private companies for owning shares in group companies. Second, the aggregate holding of all these entities taken together is typically well below a majority stake.

In many cases, the promoter may not even be the largest single shareholder. But what makes the promoters the dominant shareholders is that a large proportion of the shareholding is with state owned financial institutions that have historically played a passive role, which means that the promoters are effectively dominant shareholders and are able to get General Body approval for their actions. This is the all pervasive governance challenge for India.

ANALYSIS OF THE INDIAN OWNERSHIP PATTERNS ACROSS FIVE SECTORS

The ownership patterns across the following five sectors are analyzed for the ownership patterns and governance quality. These are:

1. Automobile sector
2. Pharmaceutical sector
3. Banking sector
4. Information Technology sector
5. Power sector

Automobile Sector

An analysis of this sector brings to light that in every large corporate in this sector that includes the top ten companies that have the highest market capitalization in this sector are all dominated by the promoter group which forms the dominant group, except in the case of Hindustan Motors where the retail investors hold a large fraction of the share holding. In the case of the Tata Group, the holding along with the total holding by all the affiliate bodies and the Tata Investment Company together holds a major holding in all the Tata concerns. Hence, in this sector the minority holding by the retail investors need the protection from the expropriation of the dominant group. Thus the process of having outsiders as monitors to supervise and align the activities of the dominant shareholders with the interest of the minority shareholders becomes highly ineffective as the appointments and nominations are all in connivance with the sanctions made by the dominant shareholder.

Pharmaceutical Sector

The Indian pharmaceutical industry is presently ranked among the best performing sectors not only in the country but, its products are finding a mark in the world markets. However, unlike the American organizations which have a diversified shareholding pattern, this sector also has a concentrated ownership holding wherein the average holding by the promoter group in all the top ten companies is an average of approximately 50 per cent and above, except in the case of Dr. Reddy's where the financial institutions have a substantial holding. This again does not take care of the agency issues between the minority and the dominant shareholder, as the interests of the financial institutions may not be aligned with the interests of the minority shareholders who look for long-term value creation, while the financial institutions may focus on short-term value creation. Hence, there could be an aggravation in conflict of interest than an alignment of the common interest. This sector again is dominated by promoter-driven ownership and control patterns where an outsider monitored governance system will be ineffective in yielding the required results.

Banking Sector

This Industry has a direct bearing on the interests of a varied section of stakeholder's. Hence this sector needs to be well governed and monitored as any misfeasance in this sector can have a contagion impact on the economy. There has been liberalization in terms of licensing granted to various business groups to commence banking operations in India. The monetary regulator plays a very active role in regulating the banking sector, and in ensuring that the banks dealing with the public funds satisfy all prudential norms as stipulated, and abide by the Basel II standards. With the opening of the banking sector private banking has taken off in a big way, with banks like ICICI bank and HDFC Bank taking lead not only in the aggressive marketing for a share of the pie, but have also taken large strides in establishing a sound governance system, for ensuring the safety and liquidity of the public money, while abiding by the rule of the land.

The banking sector barring the few large private sector banks is dominated by the public sector banks, which are required to follow the stringent and conservative norms of the RBI—the monetary regulator. The agency issue arising in

Fig. 6.1: Ownership pattern in the pharmaceutical sector

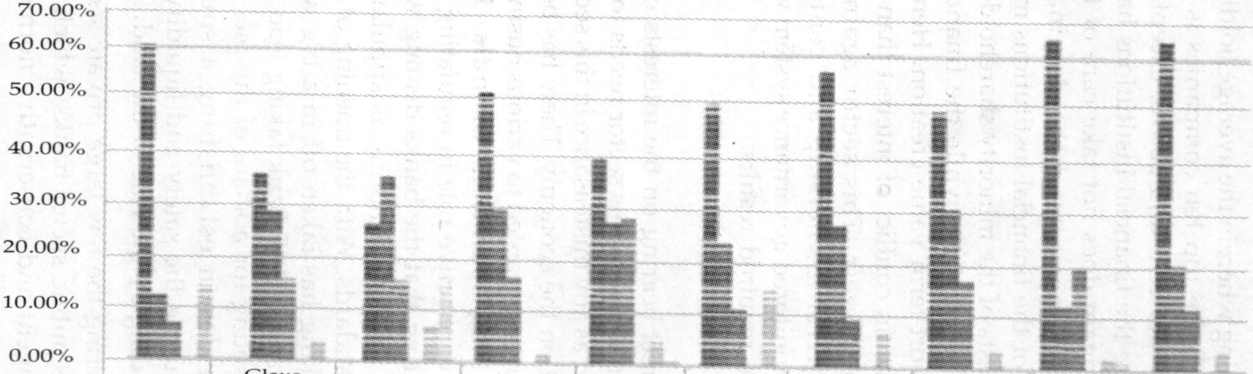

	Aventis Pharma 1	Glaxo Smithkline Pharma 2	Dr. Reddy 3	Genmark 4	Clipla Ltd. 5	Lupin Ltd. 6	Aurobindo Pharma 7	Piramal Healthcare 8	Ranbaxy Labs 9	Sun Pharma Industries 10
• Promoters	60.40%	35.90%	26.40%	52.09%	39.38%	50.63%	56.88%	49.39%	63.92%	63.71%
• Financial Institutions	12.17%	28.61%	35.75%	29.72%	27.27%	23.69%	24.47%	30.58%	12.59%	20.38%
• Retail Investors	6.87%	15.62%	15.54%	16.31%	27.75%	10.94%	9.02%	16.69%	19.77%	11.83%
• Pension Funds	0.00%	0.00%	0.00%	0.00%	0.00%	0.00%	0.00%	0.00%	0.00%	0.00%
• Mutual Funds	14.37%	3.93%	6.58%	1.88%	4.54%	14.73%	6.62%	3.35%	2.18%	4.08%
• ADR, GDRs	0.00%	0.00%	15.73%	0.00%	1.06%	0.00%	0.00%	0.00%	1.54%	0.00%

Source: Capital LINE DATA BASE, data as on 31st March 2010

organizations which are dominated by government holding are that the profitability of these businesses is often sacrificed for the socialistic goals of the government. Thereby not optimizing the resources of the investors or allocation of funds to low return securities according to the priorities set by the government. ICICI Bank leading the pack, with Yes Bank, HDFC Bank and Axis Bank has substantial stakes by institutional investors, and hence probably that is the reason they are able to play the financial games better, with large access to funding and aggressive marketing strategies.

Information Technology Sector

This sector derives its importance from the amount of foreign exchange it earns for the Indian exchequer. The industry is dominated by a few companies which have had the opportunity to access funds from the international markets. The governance of this sector has to be on line with the international benchmarks as that is the market they serve and all their business earnings depend on the service excellence that they are able to deliver to the international clients, and the quality of products that they develop. Though the sector has a large exposure to the international markets, just one company has the ownership pattern as the professional and diversified companies of US, Infosys. Infosys is the only company which stands high on governance standards and its compliance is with the Sarbanes Oxley, and several international mandates is a subject matter of consideration. All the other companies from TCS to Wipro have a concentrated shareholding pattern wherein the promoter holding far exceeds the nominal level of 51 per cent. The average holding amounts to about 65 per cent, and herein again the agency issues emerging are that of aligning the interests of the minority shareholder with that of the dominant shareholder. In most of these companies corporate governance has indeed become a ritual of tick box method, that actually ensuring that the interests of the various sections are protected.

Fig. 6.2: Ownership pattern in the Banking Sector

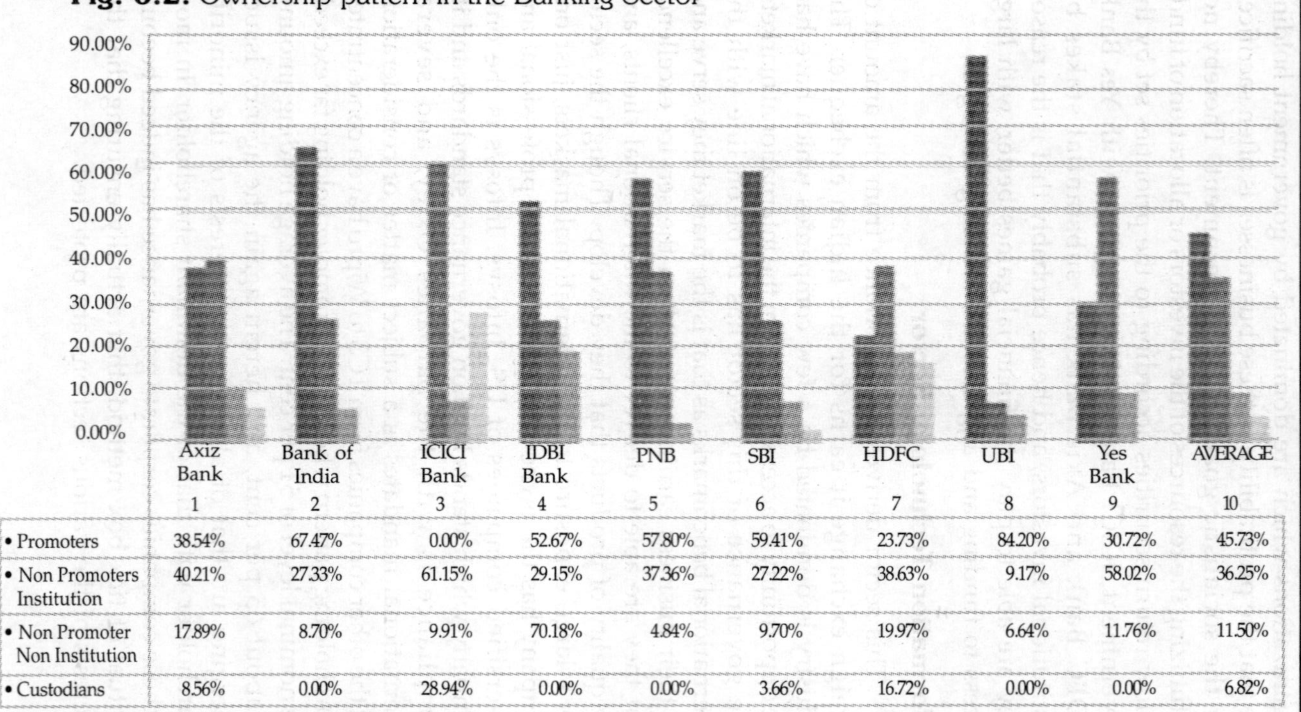

	Axiz Bank 1	Bank of India 2	ICICI Bank 3	IDBI Bank 4	PNB 5	SBI 6	HDFC 7	UBI 8	Yes Bank 9	AVERAGE 10
• Promoters	38.54%	67.47%	0.00%	52.67%	57.80%	59.41%	23.73%	84.20%	30.72%	45.73%
• Non Promoters Institution	40.21%	27.33%	61.15%	29.15%	37.36%	27.22%	38.63%	9.17%	58.02%	36.25%
• Non Promoter Non Institution	17.89%	8.70%	9.91%	70.18%	4.84%	9.70%	19.97%	6.64%	11.76%	11.50%
• Custodians	8.56%	0.00%	28.94%	0.00%	0.00%	3.66%	16.72%	0.00%	0.00%	6.82%

Source: Capital LINE DATA BASE, data as on 31st March 2010.

Power Sector

The power sector important for all infrastructural and developmental progress is crucial for the sustainable development of business in any economy. This sector calls for heavy investment, with long gestation periods, and if often funded with a large proportion of equity. The dominant players in this sector are the public sector players as the investment requirement are very huge, and the profitability will often be after a long period. Like all other sectors this sector is also dominated by the concentrated promoter holding, where in the average holding is approximately 60 per cent. This clearly brings to focus the diverse sections of minority shareholding and the protection of interests by external agencies. Independent Directors, and the external auditors have been assigned the responsibility of ensuring good governance. However when the controls are in the hands of the controlling managers, there is limited scope for the independent directors and auditors to raise their voice against these promoter groups for it is they who appoint them, and also they are the deciding authority with respect to the compensation, and reappointment.

With an overview of the ownership patterns across the various sectors, it is evident that the Indian corporate environment is different from its US counterpart and all that can bring effective governance in the American setup cannot yield the same results in the Indian environment. The differences are not only structural, but the social, political, and cultural setup requires vary widely. A recent *Financial Times* report says that Japanese companies have been told by their finance ministry that they would be foolish to rush headlong into adopting US style of corporate governance. "The American style is not universally valid as a model of improvement for Japanese companies," the finance ministry said. "Separating management and oversight and introducing external directors does not necessarily enhance corporate performance." Hideaki Miyajima, (2008) remarked "Copying just the structure of US governance does not lead to better performance". Some of the best performing Japanese

Fig. 6.3: Owership pattern in the Information Technology Sector

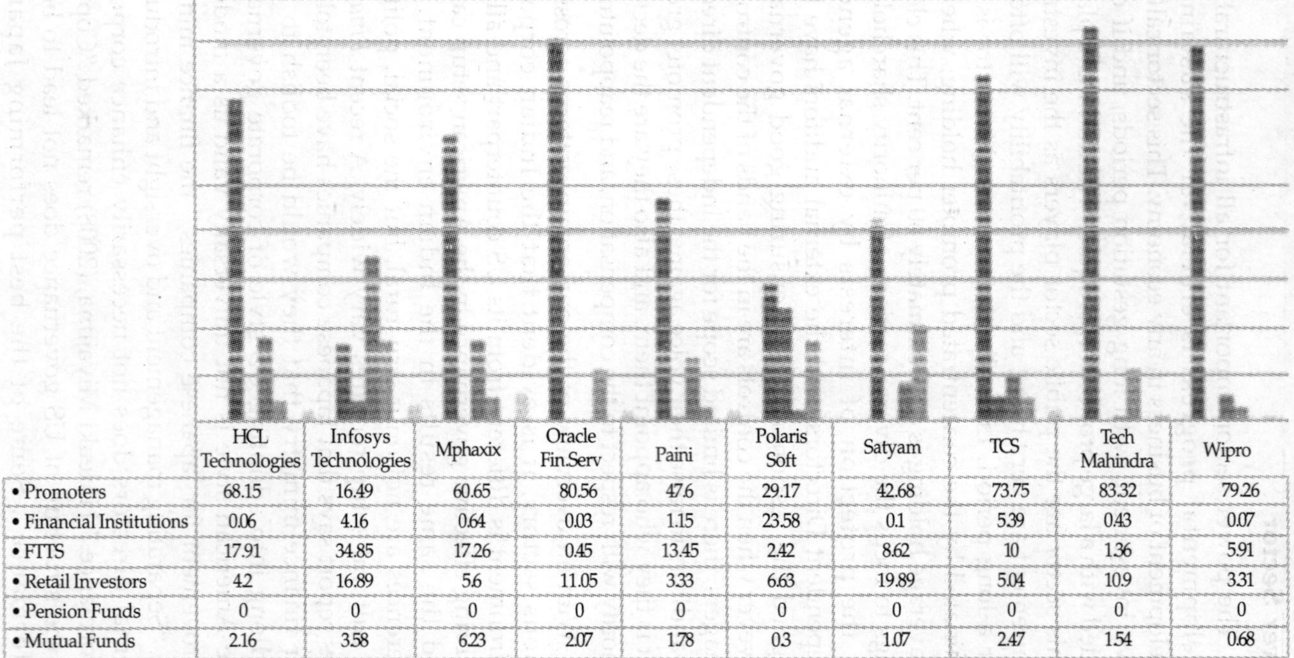

	HCL Technologies	Infosys Technologies	Mphaxix	Oracle Fin.Serv	Paini	Polaris Soft	Satyam	TCS	Tech Mahindra	Wipro
• Promoters	68.15	16.49	60.65	80.56	47.6	29.17	42.68	73.75	83.32	79.26
• Financial Institutions	0.06	4.16	0.64	0.03	1.15	23.58	0.1	5.39	0.43	0.07
• FTTS	17.91	34.85	17.26	0.45	13.45	2.42	8.62	10	1.36	5.91
• Retail Investors	4.2	16.89	5.6	11.05	3.33	6.63	19.89	5.04	10.9	3.31
• Pension Funds	0	0	0	0	0	0	0	0	0	0
• Mutual Funds	2.16	3.58	6.23	2.07	1.78	0.3	1.07	2.47	1.54	0.68

Source: Capital LINE DATA BASE, data as on 31st March 2010

companies, notably Toyota and Canon, have resisted calls to alter their governance structures radically, arguing that the US approach is inappropriate for a consensus driven society such as Japan's that strives to benefit all stakeholders.

The debate on non-executive directors is still the bone of contention for many organisations and many countries across board. Having an entire board with representations from the top level executives, and the professionals from various fields does not ensure justice to all sections of stakeholders. Indian boards need representation of employees on the board. There is so much concern for the shareholder who may hold a stock only with the primary objective of earning super-normal profits, and hammer them when the objective is not met, but employees who put a life time of service have little say in the board. Employees have a much greater stake in the long-term future of the company than the shareholders. Ultimately, a unitary board of a multinational company must have representation from each constituency i.e. shareholders, investors, employees and experts. It is now widely believed that resources contributed by stakeholders are greater than the financial investment of shareholders by a factor of ten. Employee's knowledge itself represents 70 per cent company's assets.

The refined understanding of the problem in corporate governance is largely the problem of implementation. Despite the statutory and voluntary codes there is a glaring resentment towards all compliance, and this severely hampers implementation.

For corporate governance to succeed, we have to go through a profound metamorphosis from inside out. We have to change our metaphors of success of "winner takes all" and "success at all costs" and develop an inner value system that prides on ethics, innovation, equity, legitimacy, transparency, the courage to own failures. The good news is that the role of business today is far more pervasive than ever before. Its constituency is global. For the first time in human history, the business has the power to make a difference to human lives.

Fig. 6.4: Ownership pattern in the Power Sector

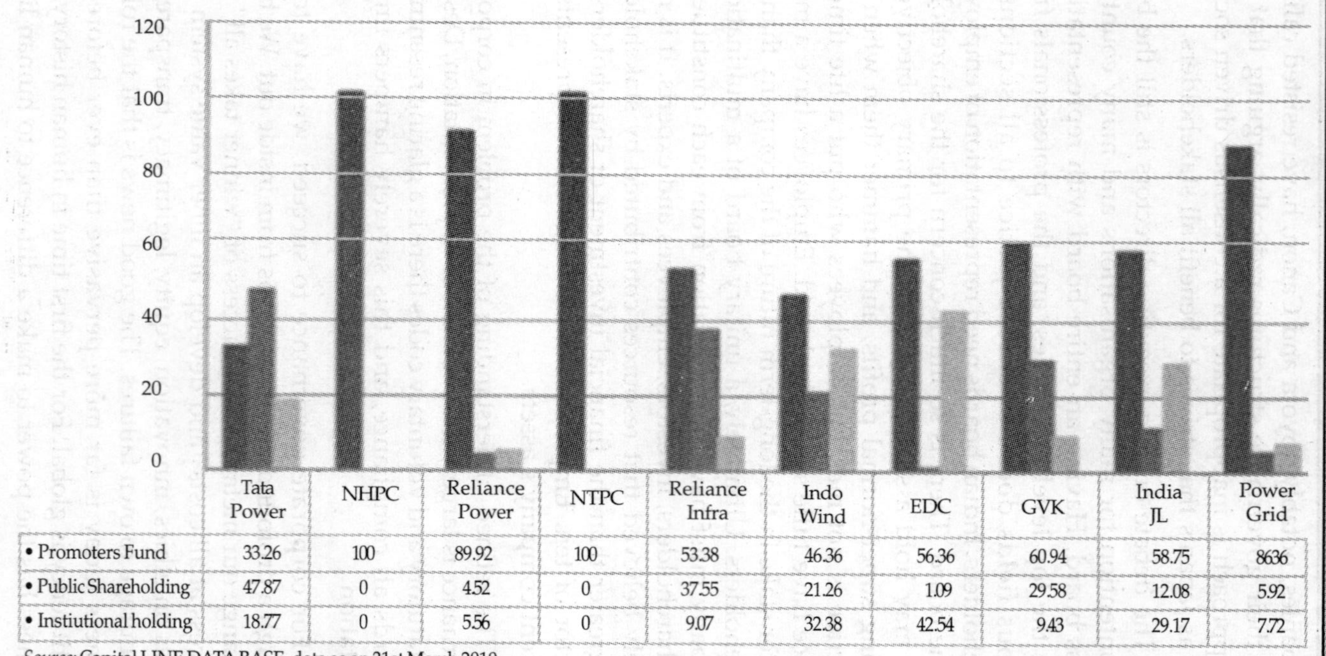

	Tata Power	NHPC	Reliance Power	NTPC	Reliance Infra	Indo Wind	EDC	GVK	India JL	Power Grid
• Promoters Fund	33.26	100	89.92	100	53.38	46.36	56.36	60.94	58.75	86.36
• Public Shareholding	47.87	0	4.52	0	37.55	21.26	1.09	29.58	12.08	5.92
• Instiutional holding	18.77	0	5.56	0	9.07	32.38	42.54	9.43	29.17	7.72

Source: Capital LINE DATA BASE, data as on 31st March 2010

Despite its failings, the business has a universal appeal. The impact that business can create in society is manifold, it is indeed business that drives politics, drives governments, aids in shaping the social values and also becoming a powerful cultural force. The political systems have not been too successful in guiding the nations on value systems. Business leaders' influence the communities to a larger extent as they impact lives directly and indirectly.

Conclusion

There has been much progress made in modernizing the stock exchanges in India; however a lot needs to be done. The most important of the glaring challenges that face the Indian Business environment is the issue of restoring confidence among small investors. One reason for the reluctance of small investors to enter the market is the low level of confidence about corporate governance in many listed companies. Information disclosures by the listed companies are way below the international standards, and are far from encouraging or conducive to the creation of market efficiency. Corporate governance standards are weak, and neither regulation nor the large institutional shareholders have succeeded in bringing about any significant improvement or strengthening of the corporate. A pre-condition for healthy capital market is the existence of institutions, which ensure high levels of corporate governance, which unfortunately is missing in the Indian environment.

Good governance calls for high standards of reporting in accountancy to ensure transparency in financial performance, active involvement of institutional investors in monitoring performance based on good quality equity research inputs and also codes of corporate governance which are designed to ensure that managements are subjected to effective oversight by boards and the shareholders interests are protected. India's capital market is as yet far from this ideal situation though some corrective processes are at work. There is a need to upgrade information through better auditing and accounting.

No amount of regulation can bring any significant improvement, unless the ethical fabric of the corporate environment gets driven by the value systems with moral conduct.

References

1. Agrawal and C. Knober. "Firm performance and mechanisms to control agency problems between managers and shareholders". *Journal of Financial and Quantitative Analysis*, 31: pp. 377-397, 1996.
2. Black, Bernard S. and Khanna, Vikramaditya S., 2007, "Can Corporate Governance Reforms Increase Firms' Market Values? Evidence from India", *Journal of Empirical Legal Studies*, Vol. 4, 2007.
3. Gautam Ahuja and Sumit K. Majumdar. An assessment of the performance of Indian State-owned enterprises. *Journal of Productivity Analysis*, 9: pp. 113 (132, 1998.)
4. IRRC, Board Practices 2000 Survey.
5. Madhav Mehra Address by the President, World Council For Corporate Governance International, *Journal for Enhancing Board Performance, Corporate Governance Moment of Truth*, 2003.
6. OECD Principles of Corporate Governance, the Responsibilities of the Board.
7. Phillip H. Phan, "The Non-Executive (Outside) Director: Key to Board Independence", in *Taking Back the Boardroom—Better Directing for the New Millennium*, McGraw-Hill, 2000.
8. Price Waterhouse-Coopers, as quoted in *The Economist*, 10 February 2001.
9. Rao, K.S. Chalapati and Pratap Chandra Biswal, "Shareholding Pattern of Listed Companies in India: Implications for Protection of Minority Shareholders' Interest", a presentation made at the International Conference: Privatization and Corporate Governance of State-owned Assets, organized by the Indian Council of Social Science Research and OECD Centre for Cooperation with Non-Member Countries, New Delhi, 27-28 November 2003.
10. Richa Mishra, K.R. Srivats (2003), "Bill soon to define 'independent directors", *The Hindu Business Line*, Feb. 23.
11. *The Economist* (2001) "The fading appeal of the Boardroom", 10 February.
12. World Bank, white paper, corporate governance in Asia 5-7 (2003).

13. Michael Jensen, "Agency Costs of Free Cash Flow, Corporate Finance, and Takeovers," *American Economic Review*, Vol. 76 (1986).

14. Renneboog Luc, *Ownership, Managerial Control and the Governance of Companies Listed on the Brussels Stock Exchange* (July 1996).

15. Van Hulle, C., 1997, The Anglo-Saxon Versus the Continental European Corporate Governance Model: Empirical Evidence of Board Composition in Belgium Congress, 287-331.

Enhancing Board Effectiveness
Role and responsibilities of CEO

Prof. Dakshayani G.N.
Prof. Nirmala Chavan

ABSTRACT

For a successful company well governed board is must. A well-functioning and effective board of directors is the Holy Grail sought by every ambitious company. A company's board is its heart and as a heart it needs to be healthy, fit and carefully nurtured for the company to run effectively. The free and accurate flow of information in and out of the board is as essential to the healthy operating of the corporate body as the free and unhindered flow of blood is to the healthy functioning of the human body. As corporations grow in size and complexity and are increasingly doing business in the global arena, it has become essential for boards to uphold the highest standards of corporate governance and to perform their role effectively. Every action taken by individuals affect the implementation process, and as can be imaged, actions taken by the top person can affect the firm's operations quite a lot. Leadership, as a consequence entails huge responsibility on the shoulders of the leaders, the CEOs of the firms. Firms have known to reach great heights just because of their CEOs. In business once it is understood that the CEO's power has great influence on the firm and its results, it becomes important and necessary to know about the power and how best it can be channeled for the maximum benefit of the firm.

The board, led, of course, by an open-minded chairman, must create the right conditions before open, honest debate will take place. Being a chairman of the board CEO has to take initiations in enhancement of board effectiveness. Even exact responsibilities of CEO vary from board to board, he has to play different roles in the company to build effective board. This paper tries to give the picture of different roles and responsibilities of CEO in enhancing the board effectiveness.

Introduction

Today, consensus is growing among industrial and transitional countries alike that economic success comes increasingly to companies, countries that provide transparent and rule of law based commercial environment. This means good business ethics, good corporate governance and effective rules, regulation, all institutions of rule of law that are attributes of today's most successful economies. We live in an age of globalization and new technology where the business environment constant flux. Because of constant change of corporate needs the corporations must be able to provide assurances that potential partners and borrowers will employ proper business practices. This will possible only if companies should have effective board and board members. Effective board should be depending of the board leadership. CEOs and board leaders recognize that an effective board must be managed, nurtured as a corporate asset and competitive differentiator. Periodic assessments of board effectiveness and governance quality are particularly important.

EFFECTIVE BOARD

The board, led, of course, by an open-minded chairman, must create the right conditions before open, honest debate will take place. The mere fact that 50 per cent of directors are independent, does not guarantee that these directors will function independently. Independent directors could be divided into three categories. First, those who are nominees of the chairman or the CEO and who perform the role of the "Nodders" in the PG Wodehouse short story of the same name—they nod whenever the chairman says anything. They are technically independent, but they echo the sentiments of the chairman and the CEO.

At the other extreme there are directors who are truly independent in the sense that they express their views clearly, fearlessly and frankly, regardless of what the chairman, or whoever has dictated their appointment, thinks. They take to heart Sam Goldwyn's famous one-liner: "I want everyone to tell me the truth, even if it costs him his job." Some have gone as far as to say that you cannot have an effective board unless constructive dissent is an accepted pattern of behavior. However many find it hard to accept that a director who disagrees with them is not trying to cast aspersions or cause harm. Dissent for its own sake is disruptive, but where, for example, directors feel that the direction being set for the company, is wrong, or a decision-making process is poor, they should not hesitate to speak out. Although it is healthy for a range of views to be aired around the board room, in the Indian context this is still the exception rather than the rule. "Many directors are afraid of looking stupid or asking a stupid question—maybe something they ought to have known—or sometimes they're afraid to confront the management."

Unless the CEO and management are receptive to outside opinion it can be very hard to articulate, let alone enforce, your point of view without offending other people. As a board director in a promoter-owned or family-owned company you don't have the ultimate sanction available to boards outside India, namely to fire the CEO if you don't agree with what he is doing. Some directors are beginning to question why they are sitting on boards where there is little discussion and scant opportunity to influence the decision-making process. The effectiveness of the board in India is influenced by several factors. Two stand out—the first is the nature of the company itself: multinationals, minority shareholder companies, public sector enterprises, group-affiliated companies and entrepreneurial businesses will expect and tolerate varying degrees of involvement by board of directors, something that should always be taken into account when considering a directorship. The second is the circumstances surrounding the appointment of board of directors. These have a marked effect on the way directors go about their duties. Directors appointed via the "old boy network" are more likely to be brought on to a board for reputational reasons rather than to provide an objective, critical perspective on key issues. To be fully effective, board of directors should prepare well for board meetings, but they must also be adequately informed and briefed about the company; only then are they in a position to comment on significant issues, including company's vision or strategy. Often a disproportionate amount of board time is spent on reviewing management presentations, leaving very little time for actual discussion among board members. It is sometimes easy for directors to become disruptive in pursuit of their statutory responsibilities. Therefore, it is critical to a company's success for directors to strike a balance between governance oversight and providing constructive support to the management. For this the effective board should consists the following components.

Components of effective board

Structuring a high performing board

(a) Define committee role, structure and composition to complete the board requirements.

(b) Select and nominate directors using a disciplined process.

(c) Evaluate the board as a whole and each director regularly.

(d) Structure the board to match the company requirements.

Ensuring effective board operations and interactions

(*a*) Makes every board meeting productive.

(*b*) Ensure the quality timeliness of all board information.

(*c*) Build trust and positive interactions dynamics.

(*d*) Open communication within the board and with management.

Fulfilling the board's fundamental roles and responsibilities

(*a*) Contributes to developing corporate strategy and set the targets.

(*b*) Upholds a string corporate performance management approach.

(*c*) Oversees development of the company future leaders and human capital.

(*d*) Understanding and manages the company risks.

(*e*) Adopts a shareholder's perspective when making decisions.

(*f*) Balance valid stakeholders interests.

With the help of this type of effective board the CEO of the company try to make balance between governance oversight and providing constructive support to the management. A close and trusting partnership between the Board and the CEO is also essential for good governance. Board members need to have enough confidence in the CEO to trust that the operational microissues are being looked after. This frees board members to concentrate on their ultimate role of looking after the "big picture". One of the worst things a board can be accused of is micromanagement—paying too much attention to detail and managing people unnecessarily, while neglecting their governance role.

THE CEO'S ROLE

In business once it is understood that CEO's power has a great influence on the firm and its results, it becomes important and necessary to know about the power and how best it can be channelized for the maximum benefit of the firm. The CEO's power can be used to influence other employees for the benefit of the firm. Hence, the CEO's personal action can be a powerful instrument for influencing strategy and bringing about organizational change. If we look at the history of the world, great men have always influenced the mass. Hitler, the evil genius, had the power to brainwash the entire German nation into believing that Jews as a race have no business to alive on the planet. His megalomaniac vision for himself as supreme, lording over the entire Europe came close to success because of his personal influence. Likewise on a different mission Mahatma Gandhi could influence the Indian nation to have a non-violent revolt against the British rule in the country. Taking a parallel, the CEO can influence his followers for achieving great and difficult objectives. It is important that both the Board and the CEO are fully aware of where their roles begin and end. If there is any confusion in an organization about roles and responsibilities, it can lead very quickly to conflict, inefficiency and low morale. It is up to the CEO to help set the agenda, assemble the information and make recommendations that shape the Board's discussions. Specifically, the CEO's tasks will include:

HRM

An effective CEO will know how to attract, retain and motivate talented and enthusiastic staff and volunteers. The CEO is also responsible for managing paid and volunteer staff according to approved personnel policies and procedures that conforms to current laws and regulations.

Planning

This involves identifying aims, objectives, strategies, responsibilities, timelines and the resources required to achieve the organisation's mission. The CEO oversees design, marketing, promotion, delivery and quality of programs, products and services. Responsibility also includes developing evaluation strategies and adjustment of systems, processes and structures in response to evaluation findings.

Financial and physical resources management

It is the CEO's responsibility to present the yearly budget for Board's approval and to manage the organisation's resources within those budget guidelines according to current laws and regulations. This includes undertaking regular risk management analyses and implementing strategies to prevent and deal with perceived risks. The Board is ultimately responsible for ensuring that these tasks are carried out to its satisfaction.

Fundraising

The CEO of a community group also oversees fund-raising planning and implementation, including identifying resource requirements, researching funding sources, establishing strategies to approach funders, submitting proposals and administering fundraising records and documentation. Again, the Board must have systems in place to ensure these things are done in a timely and effective manner.

Providing a link between the staff and the Board

It is the CEO's role to manage the staff, not the Board's. The Board should never undermine the authority of the CEO by instructing a staff member. The Board can give an order to the CEO, but not the receptionist.

Representation

The CEO needs to consistently present the organisation and its mission, programs, products and services in strong, positive images to relevant stakeholders and the general public. Board members, particularly the Chair, may also need to carry out this role occasionally, but this should generally be left up to the CEO where possible.

Setting

The Board and the CEO have a dual role in setting the standards for the organisation. This includes setting a good example when it comes to ethical behavior, loyalty, commitment, efficiency, and so on.

Vision

The CEO is responsible for creating the right internal climate for the organisation. This is something that cannot be done by the Board. An effective CEO is able to articulate the organisation's vision to staff and volunteers so that they know exactly why they do what they do—and feel great doing it.

Meetings

The CEO is responsible for ensuring that that the Board is presented with clear and logical recommendations for action; preferably well before every Board meeting to allow time for clarification and proper consideration. Most often the Board will follow the advice of the CEO and the staff, not because the Board is simply a rubber stamp but because the staff is being paid to get it right and most of the time they do. However, the CEO should not run the show; this means that the Board should be given options where there are options, not simply presented with a single decision to approve.

Ways for a CEO to Improve the Board Effectiveness

- Schedule regular meetings of the non-executive board members from which you and the other executives are excluded.
- Explain fully how discretion has been exercised in compiling the earnings and profit Figures.
- Initiate a risk-appetite review among non-executives.
- Check that non-executive directors are independent.
- Audit non-executives' performance and that of the board.
- Broaden and deepen disclosure on corporate websites and in annual reports.
- Lead by example, reining in a company culture that excuses cheating.
- Find a place for the grey and cautious employee alongside the youthful and visionary one.
- Make compensation committees independent.
- Don't avoid risk.

Areas to Play

The CEO has the following areas in which he has roles to play, where his actions can bring about the changes as dramatically as possible.

Power and influence through personal action

Personalizing the story forces CEOs to consider and share with others the answers to such questions as "Why are we changing?"; "How will we get there?"; and "How does this relate to me?". The leader of a firm uses his influence in his personal capacity and also due to his position as the CEO of the firm, on the followers in ordering the employees, making style cultural changes, persuading the employees and inducing the employees. At the ordering level, the leader is using his authority as the CEO. He can direct the board members to perform certain tasks in a given time. When it comes to changing the work system, structural changes and other cases he has to train his board members in operating new system. In case of making cultural changes he as to patiently act on revising the firm's agenda and rework the information networks with stories of success. When a CEO's version of the transformation story is clear, success comes from taking it to employees, encouraging debate about it, reinforcing it, and prompting people to infuse it with their own personal meaning.

Handling the organizational politics

The CEO must accept that politics is inevitable in every organization. In case of politics caused in the firm by clash of interests between employees that can cause a lot of damage to the firm unless it is channeled properly into creative side of the firm's activities. One-upmanship, putting others down to gain prominence in the eyes of the CEO, and competition between the employees give rise to politics. He has to use inducements in his personal capacity to set the firm's politics straight and try to have principled politics for the benefit of the firm. He can induce the members to change their ways of work and their negative thinking towards the firm. In this circumstance he should adopt open and transparency among the members. Most CEOs invest great effort in visibly and vocally presenting the transformation story. N. R. Narayana Murthy, chairman of the board and former chief executive of India's Infosys, agrees and says, "The first responsibility of a leader is to create mental energy among people so that they enthusiastically embrace the transformation."

Role as negotiator

When CEO is in the role of a negotiator he has to perform as an individual member of the firm. The most important aspect of negotiations is that the problems for which they are required cannot he wished away under the carpet. While acting as a negotiator he should need to keep the following facts:

(a) Do not negotiate on position.

(b) Create value rather than divide it by increasing the size of the cake.

(c) He should negotiate on the problem and not involve personalities of the people who are party to the negotiations.

The CEO uses his charm of persuasion when he is dealing with negations with the members; wither in the situation of members versus the firm. He also uses persuasion in communicating with the employees. Arguably the one skill today's leaders must possess is the ability to get people to agree with them. Most assuredly in any undertaking of significance, whether personal or business related, knowing how to get others to accept your point of view while seeing themselves as winners is crucial to your success, if not the prosperity of your organization. Indeed, one cannot ever expect to ascend the corporate ladder without a sound grasp of the fundamental negotiating principles and nuances or without the knowledge and skills to emulate those who consistently do it well.

Role as a communicator

One of the more pressing questions in today's emerging organisations is the key communication role of the CEO. The

CEO has to communicate the firm's vision, mission, goals and objectives, besides its plans for coping with the business environmental changes. The role of the CEO's as communicator exceeds the informative range, it goes on to listening to employees' complains, their problems which is a two way communication. Peter Drucker has maintained consistently through many decades of writing and thinking on the subject, that "the distinctive organ of organisations is management. He has long argued that the senior manager's primary responsibility is to think through the theory of his or her business and to identify the assumptions on which the organisation should base its actions. However, what needs to be emphasized is that if those assumptions are not clearly and emphatically communicated to the people who have to do the work, there will be little application of those understandings to the work done.

The modern CEO has at least two key communication roles to fulfill if he or she is to lead successfully; one is that of the motivator. He or she needs to be the chief cheerleader of the organisation. The second part of the CEO's communication job description is that of tone setter. The CEO has to be very careful about personal behaviour and personal ethics. The "don't do as I do but do as I say" approach will not work in the modern organisation. No one can preach cost-effectiveness and control and then make an exception of himself. While a definitive and widely accepted profile and/or description of the CEO role is hard to find, it's possible to describe the communication elements of that role. The CEO and senior leadership team must see the big picture, clarify, focus and communicate it. They must connect the organization to the outside world, set goals and chart the path to the future. They must communicate externally with diverse stakeholders, including the financial community, civic interests, customers and the public as a whole; while internally, leadership must inform and let employees know the part they'll play in the organization's success.

Role of being a role model

CEO in a firm is looked upon as a role model whom the employees try to emulate, subconsciously attempting to get into his shoes. Whether leaders realize it or not, they seem to be in front of the cameras when they speak or act. "Every move you make, everything you say, is visible to all. Ultimately, employees will weigh the actions of their CEO to determine whether they believe in the story. Employees expect the CEO to live up to Mahatma Gandhi's famous edict, "For things to change, first I must change." The CEO is the organization's chief role model. As a role model the CEO has act in different roles. They are

(a) catalyst for transformation.

(b) reaching out to the entire firm's administration.

(c) planner of strategies.

(d) problem solver.

As the catalyst for transformation, it is his actions, which create the right ambience in the firm, leading to the desired changes, as the employees look up to him for not guidance but also inspiration and direction. While in the administration CEO has to assure the members of fairness in dealing related to them. He has to prepare strategies and ensure that they are executed to perform to perfection and in time. As a problem solver he must become a good listener to understand the problem thoroughly. Having a large heart the CEO would concentrate on the bigger picture and ignore minor pinpricks to keep free from getting bogged down with these minor problems.

Corporate image builder

There are four desired images that CEOs can use to integrate their organisation's internal activities, and to coordinate these with its external communications to project a desired image. These are: 'Pathfinder', 'Commander', 'Change', and 'Vision'. As a pathfinder CEO he build the corporate image of the company by taking leadership. As a commander his role is rational analyst, while adopting changes he act as an architect and at the time of achieving the vision of the company he act as coordinator or mentor. The role of pathfinder CEOs is to convince other people that their dream is worthwhile following. Extensive analysis of the environment, market conditions, and competitors is to be undertaken before any action is taken to change the desired image of the organization. Here the CEO is an architect who uses the resources and control mechanisms of the organisation to establish a taskforce to examine its current images and to recommend the next course of action for change. As a catalyst for building an organisation's desired reputation, the vision statement must be 'sold' throughout the organisation by the CEO.

Planner/strategist

As a planner or strategist the CEO's role is achieve the missions, to define organizational goals and formulate strategy. In organizational development he has to Determine skills and competencies needed for mission accomplishment and develop organizational structure. As a to strategist he has set the performance standards by establishing the performance standards needed to ensure mission accomplishment, for effective and efficient use of resources he should develop work processes and controls that will provide efficient operations and prevent unauthorized use of resources. Lastly as a planner and strategist of the board he should give administrative support to the Board by organizing and planning its work.

As a administrator/ supervisor

As a good administrator he should plan and assign work, delegate accountability for accomplishment of organizational goals. To develop organizational structure he should hire, train, and coach workforce. Develop the competencies needed to accomplish the measure and evaluate performance. For effective and efficient use of resources he should authorize work and adopt supervise operations by monitoring and evaluating financial expenditure. To perform board activities he has to provide staff assistance to the board as an administrator.

CEO's Responsibilities towards the Board

The work of the chief executive is to manage the corporation. It is distinct and separate from the work of governance. Typical chief executive responsibilities define what the chief executive must do. The following are typical CEO responsibilities but not necessarily the only ones:

- Achieving the mission
- Organizational development
- Setting performance standards
- Effective and efficient use of resources
- Providing administrative support for the board
- Timely communication with the Board on financial and administrative matters
- Effective representation of the company to enhance its public image
- Prompt and thoughtful response to Board requests for information

Conclusion

Every move you make, everything you say, is visible to all. Therefore the best approach is to lead by example.

The description of the work of the CEO demonstrates how much he contributes to the performance of the corporation. High performance organizations exhibit strong teamwork between the board and corporate management. Good board governance empowers effective management action. For this CEO has put effort in making the transformation meaningful, modeling the desired mind-sets and behavior, building a strong and committed team, and relentlessly pursuing impact. Together, these can powerfully generate the energy needed to achieve a successful performance transformation. As leaders in business, the CEOs through their actions can influence the strategic implementation process. They have to resort to using their authority in their individual capacity for persuading and inducing the employees. The best way to achieve success is to combine the two personal charisma and official authority to influence the employees to bring about the desired change. Most CEOs invest great effort in visibly and vocally presenting the transformation story. R. Narayana Murthy, chairman of the board and former chief executive of India's Infosys, agrees and says, "The first responsibility of a leader is to create mental energy among people so that they enthusiastically embrace the transformation. The CEOs must accept the firm's politics as a part of the system. Playing healthy politics, which is transparent and value based, can, in fact, go in favor of the firm. The CEO has to negotiate on a number of issues, with the workers, board member and in dispute between employees. The CEO's effectiveness depends on how best he can communicate with his board members. The content and the method of communication both are equally important. Effective communication depends on the power of listening, to understand their problems before the CEO attempts to solve them. The CEO must project himself through his actions that he is a role model, worthy of emulation by others. The respect and faith he generates with his board member and employees helps the firm to tide over difficult situations, helps it in affecting organizational changes and making it a fully learning organization.

References

1. *Corporate governance and business ethics—text and cases*, U.C. Mallur.
2. *Corporate governance and accountability*, Wiley Publications.
3. Axelrod, Nancy R., *The Chief Executive's Role in Developing The Nonprofit Board*, The National Centre for Nonprofit Boards, 1988.
4. Nason, John W., *Board Assessment of the Chief Executive: A Responsibility Essential to Good Governance*, National Center for Nonprofit Boards, Washington, DC, 1990.

5. Cornforth, Chris and Edwards, Charles, *Good Governance-Developing Effective Board-Management Relations in Public and Voluntary Organisations,* The Chartered Institute of Management Accountants, 1998, London.

6. "The Conference Board Task Force on Executive Compensation," September 21, 2009, http://www.conference-board.org/pdf_free/ExecCom-pensation2009.pdf.

7. The McKinsey Quarterly: The Online Journal of McKinsey and Co. http://www.mckinseyquarterly.com/article_print. aspx?L2=21&L3=0&ar=1912.

8. N.R. Narayana Murthy Committee Report, 2003.

9. Gopalswamy N., *Corporate Governance the new Paradigm,* Wheeler Publishing, New Delhi 1008.

Corporate Governance
Is it justified

C. Chandra Shekar Reddy

ABSTRACT

The very objective of any corporate sector is to earn the return over the investment. In this direction, the leadership plays vital role. The success or failure of a corporate firm to a greater extent depends on the leadership. Leadership is the process of influencing the people's behavior towards the goal realization. The leader is one who leads the followers, trains the employees working in the organization to achieve the desired goals. A leader should have vision to land the organization in a better place than the competitors as per the goals set in. The corporate sector aims to excel through effective leadership by adopting professionalism in management. A leader must have foresight and able to predict uncertainties that influence the performance of a firm and be prepared to absorb the shocks that are likely to arise due to uncertainty. The leader is expected to motivate the employees, create the environment and extract maximum out of available human resources. The leader is expected to create conducive environment where employees work wholeheartedly with commitment and dedication. A leader must have clarity on the goals of the organization, communicate to the lower level employees working in the organization, possess effective managerial abilities and delegate authority to the individual divisions. To make the delegation more effective the leader has to define the terms like, authority, responsibility and accountability.

The purpose of this paper is to integrate the bases of power and measure the level of motivation among the employees working in the organization i.e., effectiveness of the situational leadership. To measure the motivation levels of leadership, it is proposed to study the effectiveness of leadership by using the parameters namely, expert, information, referent, legitimate, reward, connection and coercion. The data would be collected from both sources i.e., primary and secondary. Suitable questionnaire will be designed and administered among the employees working in few corporate. Appropriate statistical tools will be applied to analyze the data.

Keywords: Corporate Sector, employees, motivation, leadership, accountability.

What is Corporate Governance?

"Corporate governance is the system by which business corporations are directed and controlled. The corporate governance structure specifies the distribution of rights and responsibilities among different participants in the corporation, such as, the board, managers, shareholders and other stakeholders and spells out the rules and procedures for making decisions on corporate affairs. By doing this, it also provides the structure through which the company objectives are set and the means of attaining those objectives and monitoring performance", OECD April 1999, OECD's definition is consistent with the one presented by Cadbury (1992, page 15).

Transparency and Accountability

In a crispy term, corporate governance can be understood as the process which enables "Enhancement of the return on capital through increased accountability". It is, in fact, the mechanism by which values; principals, management policies and procedures of a company are made in consonance with the real world. It refers to the entire system by which the company is managed and monitored in a transparent manner. Undoubtedly, transparency and accountability are considered as the two fundamental principles for good corporate governance. In a practical sense, corporate governance provides a structure through which the objectives of the organizations are achieved and the performance monitored from time to time.

Corporate governance has several claimants—shareholders and other stakeholders include suppliers, customers, creditors, bankers, and employees of the company, the government and the society at large. The right starting point for good corporate governance is the high degree of priority on the interests of the shareholders who have immense faith in the Corporations to use the investment funds wisely and effectively.

Corporate governance, therefore, is only part of the larger and economic context in which the funds of the shareholders operate. However, sustenance and long-term success of a company depends on the factors such as business ethics and corporate awareness of the environmental and societal interest of the communities in which it operates. The degree to which corporations observes the basic principles of good corporate governance is considered increasingly as an important factor.

Ethical Standards

According to N. R. Murthy, "Rules cannot substitute for character. It is ethical behaviour that will ensure that the CEO and the internal members of the board or the senior management behave properly. Decent and desirable behaviour goes beyond the domain of rules that are mandated. Remember that the rule of law cannot defeat the perversity of the heart".

Internal Controls

In the Indian context, the importance of internal control has been emphasized to a greater extent in the corporate sector. For instance, N. R. Murthy has emphasized the importance of internal control as: "It is important for companies to have effective internal controls in order to ensure good corporate governance standards. The annual report should contain a report of the audit committee on their satisfaction of the measures taken during the period to strengthen such internal controls. Right now, in India, this is mandated only for listed companies. However, we should extend this to include the subsidiaries of public companies as well". While governments play a central role in shaping the legal, institutional and regulatory climate within which individual corporate governance systems are developed, the main responsibility lies with each corporation.

Corporate Governance framework usually encompasses the following Board of Directors/Board Committees

- Management Information System
- Risk Management Framework
- Internal Control Mechanism
- Whistleblower Policy
- Disclosure of Information
- Code of Conduct for Employees

What is Whistleblowing?

Whistleblowing can be defined in a number of ways. In its simplest form, whistle blowing involves the act of reporting wrong doing within an organization to internal or external parties. Internal whistle blowing entails reporting the information to a source within the organization. External whistleblowing occurs when the whistleblower takes the information outside the organization, such as to the media or regulators.

Who is a Whistleblower?

Whistleblower is a person who reports against corruption or any other such malpractices or perceived unethical organizational practices etc which take place in organization whether private or governmental to an internal authority or outside authorities such as press, government, public interest groups.

Famous Whistleblowers

Cynthia Coopers, an internal auditor and consultant who is best-known for being the whistleblower who exposed massive accounting fraud at WorldCom in 2002. Cooper worked as the Vice President of Internal Audit at WorldCom. After conducting a thorough investigation in secret, she informed the audit committee of WorldCom's board that the company had covered up $3.8 billion in losses through phony bookkeeping. At the time, this was the largest incident of accounting fraud in U.S. history.

Sherron Watkins was Vice-President of Corporate Development at the Enron Corporation, helped to uncover the Enron scandal in 2001.She wrote a concerned internal email message to Enron CEO Kenneth Lay pointing out that there were mis-statements in the financial reports.

Satyendra Kumar Dubey project director at the National Highways Authority of India accused his employer in a letter to the then Prime Minister Atal Behari Vajpayee.

Social Responsibility towards Different Interest Groups

Even though corporate responsibility for increasing the wealth of owners (shareholders) is well recognized, other social responsibilities are only beginning to be accepted. A brief list of the many areas is given here, in which corporations have acknowledged their social responsibility and established programmes to deal with them.

(i) Natural environment: Responsibility for protecting the natural environment includes judicious use of natural

resources, energy conservation, abatement of polluting emissions, and waste management.

(ii) Consumers: Responsibility towards consumers includes production of safe items and using biodegradable packages, educating consumers on product use and disposal, being truthful in advertising, and establishing a procedure for dealing with consumer complaints.

(iii) Employees: Responsibility towards employee welfare includes providing fair compensation and benefits and safe work environment, eliminating discrimination, providing opportunities for personal and professional development, and having progressive human resource policies.

(iv) Government agencies: Responsibilities toward local, state and central government agencies include fulfilling obligations under regulations and statutes of these agencies, cooperating in planning and investigations, and coordinating administrative activities with these agencies.

(v) Community: Responsibilities to the public or communities where the corporation has operations include providing economic stability, safeguarding public safety, protecting the environment, and aiding in the development of social and cultural resources of the community through corporate philanthropy.

(vi) Media: Responsibilities toward the media include being cooperative and truthful about issues that affect public welfare.

Corporate Governance is not merely about preparing 'corporate governance report' to comply with listing agreement. It is not merely forming various committees.

Basically, Corporate Governance is about ethics in business. Ethics cannot be legislated. It is about transparency, openness and fair play in all aspects of business operations.

Much like "quality" in the '80s, "ethics" and "integrity" have become business buzzwords, materializing in too many CEO internal communications and speeches. Many well-

STAKEHOLDERS
• SHAREHOLDERS safety for Investment & Equitable Returns
• AUTHORITIES Compliance of Regulations.
• COMPETITORS Healthy Competition
• Suppliers Fair Deals & Long Term
EMPLOYEES
• Equal Opportunity Employer.
• Provision of Social Security.
• Taking care of Health, Safety & Welfare Needs.
• Wellness Programmes.
• Retirement Planning.
• Dependents Care
• Employee Empowerment.
• Gender Equality.
• Empolyment for Disabled.
• Elimination of Child Labour.
CUSTOMERS
• Right to Information.
• Fair Deals.
• Wider Choice.
• Innovative Products.
• Customer Satisfaction.
• After Sales Service
• Ethical Standards in Advertising.
• Understanding Social & Environmental Impact of Products.
• Addressing Customer Redressal/Grievances.
Business Unit's Responsibility towards
GOVERNMENT
• Compliance of Tax Laws and Regulations
Summary
• Investment in Science and Technology.
• Fostering Ethical Trade Practices.
• Transparency in Business Deals
• Generating Revenues
SOCIETY
• Respecting Human Rights
• Provision of Employment
• Contribution to National Income
• Striving for Social and Economic Progress.
• Involvement in Sustainable Development Programs
• Sharing Resources with Underprivileged Communities.
• Funding Social Activities.
• Promotion of Healtcare/ Education/Rural Infrastructure.
ENVIRONMENT
• Conservation of Energy
• Usage of Non-Conventional Resources
• Adoption of Environment friendly Technologies.
• Preservation of Biodiversity Treatment of Waste before Disposal
• Train Staff in Environmental Issues.
• Increase Product Life & Minimize Packaging.
• Use Recyced & Reclable Products.

intentioned and well-educated people think this "ethical emphasis" is a healthy development. The fundamental challenge of business ethics is that there are legitimately competing values for determining an appropriate course of action. These competing values are particularly contentious when running a bigger business unit. A sense of ethical obligation is to be created. This refers to the intuitive or learned understanding that ethical fibers—a concern for fairness, justice, and due process to people, groups, and communities should be woven into the fabric of managerial decision-making. However, the governments also have to create the regulatory framework, but it can at most ensure the formalities of Corporate Governance are complied with. It has to come through conviction and self-discipline of top management. Otherwise, it remains an empty formality. So companies should adopt Corporate Governance in letter and spirit as well. Thus, what is needed a small corpus of legally mandated rules, buttressed by a much larger body of self-regulation and voluntary compliance.

The managements and leaders of business must internalise the values of ethical management as articulated by Norman Vincent Peale and Kenneth Blanchard. As the *Chandokya Upanishad* says: If we apply knowledge with faith, dedication and deep analysis, our actions become stronger. This will lead to success.

CASE STUDY OF SATYAM

Coming to the latest Satyam issue which gave rise to this whole debate on corporate governance. The companies, which were the darlings of the stock market and held up as models for vigorous and innovative growth can ultimately collapse like a house of cards as they were based on fraud and dishonesty.

Reasons Quoted for Satyam Fiasco

Mr. Ramalingaraju adopted highly centralized, top down approach.

Board of directors under seize.

Concealed Audit system.

Loopholes in the system.

Questions to be raised and my probable solutions to be discussed in the presentation.

Is Satyam is the actual problem?

Actually Satyam is not the problem, it is only the consequence affected by corporate governance failure in India. May be Infosys or Wipro have Satyams underlied in them. Nothing can be guaranteed in the present Governance conditions.

Is Satyam is the only scandal?

Satyam can't be told as only scandal, may be Infosys or Wipro have Satyams underlied in them. Nothing can be guaranteed in the present Governance conditions.

Should Govt review Satyam and Bailout it?

Why should this happen, why should general peoples money should be invested in the private company by the government of India?

If the government want to bailout Satyam there will be many companies, many no of employees will come with same aspect in the future then what will be government position.

How Mr. Ramlingaraju to be punished?

Mr. Ramlingaraju approached clever technique of surrendering himself in the peak time. He is safe under bars, then what about the stakeholders outside.

Role of the Auditors

However, good financial reporting is not a sufficient condition for the effectiveness of corporate governance if users don't process it, or if the informed user is unable to exercise a monitoring role due to high costs. A system of good Corporate Governance promotes relationship of accountability between the principal actors of sound financial reporting—the board, the management and the auditor. It holds the management accountable to the board and the board accountable to the shareholders. The Audit Committee's role flows directly from the board oversight function. It acts as a catalyst for effective financial reporting.

The scorecard of the auditors in this regard is not so much satisfactory in the pre-globalisation era. Though the law provides enough check and balance to ensure the independence of the auditors to enable them to maintain professional objectivity in performing their duties, the role of auditors are still way behind the standard. One of the reasons cited for this situation is that the auditors do not want to bite the hands which feed them. According to the Companies Act, the shareholders are the appointing authority of the auditors. However in practice, the amorphous shareholders never propose the name of auditors to the annual general meeting. It is only the management which proposes the name to the AGM and thence to the annual general meeting by the Board. The intimacy of the relationship to the management is vastly stronger than to the shareholders.

The present day auditor's duty is complete with a mere attachment of a note. They are not interested in the welfare of the shareholders. Perhaps the fear of not being reappointed by clients, some auditors may hesitate to state their observations. Their contention is that the auditors are expected only to express the opinion of the truth of the financial statements prepared by the management and they are not supposed to carry out a proprietary audit. Small group dynamics tend to make them agree with each other and to forget their role representing outside interests. Though the auditing professionals are not prepared to let the MNC Audit firms, they have assimilated some of the practices of the MNC firms. In the pre-globalisation era, qualified reports were very rare to find even if it is needed for a sample study purpose. Now the qualified reports are started appearing regularly, thanks to the change in the role perception of the auditors and their perception about their independence.

References

1. Edition (August 2001) Balchandran, S (2005), Ethics, *Indian Ethos and Management*, Shroff Publishers, pp 48-50.
2. Aga, Anu R. (2004), *Embracing CSR*, Forum of Free Enterprises, Mumbai.
3. "Corporate Governance Panel Moots Whistle Blower Policy" *Business Line*, Dec. 16, 2003.
4. *HRD newsletter*, publication of the HRD network, January 2008.
5. "India needs a Whistle Blower Protection Act" *The Hindu*, Mar 25th 2003
6. A. A. S. Ranasinghe *"Whistle-blowing-A failure of organisational culture"*?

Ethical Code of Conduct

An essential ingredient in corporate governance

Prof. Dakshayani, G.N.

ABSTRACT

Organizations adopt ethical corporate codes because they want to regulate themseives in order to avoid government regulations and this is a strategy adopted to improve their image with general public and their peers in the industry. The term corporate code is usually interchangeable with codes of practice and code of conduct. Corporate ethics', which had low profile in corporate world, has suddenly gained status. In fact, the word 'ethics' was considered irrelevant by corporate loyalists, but now is critical to a company's success. The intensity of consumer movements, the entry of MNCs in the Indian market and the raising level of awareness among corporate stakeholder are making it difficult for corporate to get away with unethical governance practices. Corporate governance is the most chanted mantra of 21st century business leader. This paper explores dimensions relating to ethics and the need of code of conduct in corporate governance and the basic obligations of the directors/management.

Introduction

As market forces increasingly replace government controls, corporate governance is fast gaining prominence in business circles. The issue of corporate governance has become a matter of concern for corporations as they see it as a prerequisite for attracting funds from foreign financial institutions. In other words the issue of corporate governance is an issue of agency function namely how to ensure that the interests of the investors are taken care of. This is not only in terms of return on investment by effective management but also ensuring that the enterprises don't indulge in corrupt practices or acts, which are ethical. Now Indian corporates are realizing that integrity, transparency and open communications are the new norms of the corporate world. 'Corporate ethics' had low profile in corporate world, has suddenly gained status. In fact the word 'ethics' was considered irrelevant by corporate loyalists, but now it is critical to a company's success.

At first glance, it may seem that for more use can be made of a Code of Conduct. After all, such a Code provides clear and unambiguous direction about appropriate standards of behavior. However, further examination of the issue reveals that the less specific Code of Ethics is the more significant.

While a Code of Ethics is the better vehicle for ensuring long-term commitment to important values. This is because a Code of Ethics demands something more than mere compliance. Instead, such a Code calls forth exercises in understandings that is linked to a requirement that people exercise judgment and accept personal responsibility for the decisions that they make.

Relevance of Ethics

"The fundamental objective of corporate governance is the enhancement of long-term shareholder value while at the same time, protecting the interests of other stakeholders".

—*Kumar Mangalam Committee Report of Corporate Governance, 1999.*

"We've always striven hard for respectability, Transparency and to create an ethical organization. There are certain expectations that we haven't fulfilled. But were also a very young organization and in areas like track record of management, we may be low because we're yet to show longevity".

—Narayana NR Murthy,
Chairman and CEO,
Infosys Technologies Limited (Infosys), 2001.

The incorporation of code of conduct in corporate governance is the basic obligations of the directors/management. When it comes to creating an ethical culture, it is important to note that the focus of ethical thinking is an indispensable tool for those who encounter a constant stream of new challenges in a rapidly changing world. Corporate performance ultimately depends on the consistent application of a founding set of values and principles as code of conduct.

Corporate governance practices are a set of structural arrangements that are emerging in free marketing economics to align the management of companies with the interest of their shareholders in particular and other stakeholders and society at large. Many factors have contributed to the evolution of ethical corporate governance, some of these are:

- For ensuring good corporate conduct which has shifted from government and to free marketing economy.
- To active participation of individual and institutional investors.
- Increasing competition in global economy.

Issue in Corporate Governance

Corporate governance addresses three basic issues—Ethical issues, Efficiency issues and Accountability issues.

Ethical issues are concerning with the problem of fraud, which is becoming wide spread in the capitalistic economy.

Efficiency issues are concerned with the performance of management.

Accountability issues are emerges out of the stakeholders need for transparency of management in the conduct of business.

Therefore ensuring better corporate performance through involvement in the strategy formulation and policy making, corporate conformance through top management supervision and accountability to the stakeholders come under the ambit of corporate governance.

Corporate Codes

Every organization whether large or small, has its own corporate code. Corporate codes reflect the purpose of the company and guide the employee to behave in an ethical manner. For some years now, the topic of ethics has been gaining increased exposure across the ranks of the management community, its advisors and regulators.

A code of ethics express fundamental principles of guidance in cases where no specific rule is in place or where matters are genuinely unclear. A well drafted code of conduct will be consistent with the primary code of ethics. However, it will provide much more specific guidance. In comparison to a code of conduct, a code of ethics will trend to be more general, contain fewer principles, be expressed in term of 'ought' or 'should', Be directed to all personal affected, provide general guidance in those where a code of conduct is silent and ambiguous or unclear.

Provisions in the Code of Ethics

- That our actions should be based on recognition of the essential dignity of each and every person.
- That we should have an active concern for the well being of the community and the environment.
- That we should provide a challenging and safe workplace in which people can flourish.

Why Codes Fail?

Putting it bluntly, even well-intentioned people are committed to the folly of developing codes as an alternative to the active and creative management of an organization's culture. At first glance the solution seems to be relatively cheap and efficient. In fact, it is regrettably common for the following process to unfold:

1. refer the matter of 'ethics' to Corporate Counsel, Human Resources or a consultant.
2. have the appointed individual draft an appropriate document (usually based on earlier attempts by others).
3. publish the code (occasionally with a 'sign off' requirement).
4. activate the internal monitoring/enforcement regime.
5. sit back and relax.

This is, of course, something of a caricature. However, when it comes to addressing the 'problem of ethics', most companies look for a cheap 'off the shelf' solution. What is more, those who seek such a solution do so in the face of compelling evidence that solutions of this type may be superficially efficient—but almost totally ineffective. This is because broader issue of ethics is set aside in favor of the 'hard science' of specifying types of behavior that, in defined situations, are to be prescribed or proscribed.

Implementation of Corporate Codes

Implementation of Corporate Codes based on four aspects:

- Organizational structure : Appropriate delegation of authority.
- Co-ordination : Among different departments.
- Motivation : Motivating employees through the quality of ethical performance of their company.
- Communication : Effective co-ordination and motivation of employees aim at maintaining ethical climate.

Pre-requisites for Proper Implementation

Draw the Baseline through values audit

Few organizations should take the trouble to assess the culture that they seek to reinforce or change to develop an approach to the organization's ethos through conducting a 'values audit'. A survey will help to identify what people think to be important of value, believe to be the ideal level presence of each value. But this exercise will start to identify the 'values gap'. This audit will provide a base line against which progress can be assessed.

Involvement through participation

It is still important to observe that people are more likely to apply rules that they have had a hand in developing than those which have been handed down i.e. ownership of a process can create an acknowledged *prima facie* obligation. This naturally works to the advantage of those who look for compliance. The fact that a company chooses to encourage its entire people to participate in defining its ethos indicates that personnel are regarded as being more than mere means for securing the organization's ends to open culture. Suggesting that the process should be extended from the board-room to the factory floor suggesting an open culture.

Realistic short development cycles

On the practical front, the quicker the turn-around, the greater the likelihood that positive reinforcement can be achieved. Otherwise less of a concern to provide timely reports of the findings make people become cynical and easily develop the perception that the entire exercise was nothing more than a 'gesture' by management.

Built-in-review

Codes come to be seen as stale or 'set in stone' losing their immediacy and relevance. Leading to the code is likely to fail in its application.

Managers need to surrender responsibility

It is reasonable for managers to extent the decision-making process by involving their colleagues and to specify that they have to accept the responsibility for making the final decisions. This suggests a commitment to principles of workplace democracy.

Role of Directors

Directors should have the capacity to—

- Recognize the need for a properly developed corporate philosophy and ethos.
- Stimulate the development and articulation of a corporate philosophy and ethos.
- Ensure that there is a proper appreciation of the importance of managing the values.
- Ensure that the institutional design of the organization under their direction is such that it reinforces the values that it purports to represent.
- Provide considered advice and assistance in the debate and resolution of ethical issues and dilemmas that arise from time to time.

Ethical Code of Conduct—Role of Board

There are four key principles:

1. There is a need for commitment from the top, and that means from the board and senior managers. Not just a verbal nod, but a real commitment. Unless that happens people will be justified in asking questions about the level of sincerity lying behind the development of an organization's ethics.
2. It will be useful to document the agreed values of an organization. Such a document will set out the fundamental principles which people are going to hold to. Codes are very important documents—a bit like the Ten Commandments, in that they make sure that important principles are kept.
3. There also needs to be a commitment to review the code continually.

4. The organization has to be aware of any 'blockages' that may prevent an accumulated store of commitment and goodwill from actually working to the benefit of the organization.

How to Make the Codes Work?

Taking into consideration the difference between the two types of code and bearing in mind the earlier discussion about the ways in which common approaches to developing these codes can lead to failure. The only thing that might prevent them from being labeled as the fruit of common sense is the fact that they are so uncommonly applied in practice.

Conclusion

If an organization is to flourish, especially in times of change, then it must manage its values and principles in a way that provides a stable foundation for growth and development.

To conclude we quote an example of high priest of Corporate Governance—'Infosys benchmark whether corporate governance made infosys one of the most admire companies in India was its corporate governance practices. Infosys believe in commitment to values, ethical conduct of business and making a clear distinct between personal and corporate funds. Complied with most of the recommendations made by CII (Confederation of Indian Industries). The recipient of many awards for Business world -IMRB survey, the company that other try to Emulate by *Economic Times* survey. It can be said that Infosys corporate governance ethical practices has offered many lessons to corporate India.

To conclude, it can be said that a Code of Ethical conduct should not be a substitute for personal responsibility; rather, code should be an authentic expression of what people hold to be right and proper.

As a final point, it should be stressed that there is no formula for developing a true set of ethical principles that will guide a company. It is unfortunate, but true that there is no 'quick fix' when it act ethically. But there is no way to inherent part of life in all its dimensions.

References

1. The Institute of Company Secretaries of India (2004): *Coporate Governance (Modules of Best practices).*
2. Josesph W Weiss, *Business Ethics: A stakeholder and issue management approach,* 3rd Edition.
3. O.C. Ferrel, John Paul Fraedrich, Linda Ferrell (2008) *Business Ethics Ethical Decision Making and Cases,* Sixth Edition, Biztantra.
4. P.S. Bajaj, Dr. Raj Agarwal (2008): *Business Ethics: An Indian Perspective,* Biztantra Publication.
5. Pearson, A (1992), "Corporate Redemption and the Seven Deadly Sins" in *The Harvard Business Review,* May-June 1992.
6. Labich, K (1992), 'The New Crisis in Business Ethics' in *Fortune International,* 20 April 1992. Business world, September 24, 2001.
7. Suzenne Ross (2004), "Universal Values Do they exist? Can one code fit all?" published in *Living Ethics,* Issue 61.
8. Dunlop, Sir John, (1987), "The Responsibility of Company Director: Formulation of the Major Policies of the Company" in *Dunlop on Directors,* Sydney, the Institute of Directors in Australia.

Current Issues in Good Corporate Governance

Deo Vinayak, S.
Tammewar, Mamta S.
Mr. Mudholkar, G.P.

ABSTRACT

Corporate governance mechanisms affect firm value, market liquidity and the organization of industries and markets in a context of weak shareholder protection. Controlling-shareholders divert resources for their own consumption, in turn reducing shareholder value. Given the potential to large private benefits of control, I also explore the motivation for outside investors to participate in the financing of the firm's activities. The results of the investigation will shed light on the question of how much (private consumption) is too much. Furthermore, we extend the literature on the interactions between several governance mechanisms and firm value. Corporate governance mechanisms affect firm value, market liquidity and the organization of industries and markets in a context of weak shareholder protection. One of the focal points of the corporate governance literature is the role of the ownership structure as a governance mechanism. According to one of the traditional finance paradigms, the ownership of public corporations is widely dispersed among atomistic investors. Even in the US, controlling-shareholders govern a large number of firms. A concentrated ownership structure gives rise to a new form of conflict of interest: between controlling shareholders and minority-shareholders. The conflict of interest is characterized as the potential for asset diversion from the firms to the controlling-shareholders, reducing overall shareholders' value.

Introduction

The Organization for Economic Cooperation and Development (OECD), which in 1999 published its Principles of Corporate Governance offers a more detailed, definition of corporate governance as "the internal means by which corporations are operated and controlled, which involve a set of relationships between a company's management, its board, its shareholders and other stakeholders Corporate Governance also provide the structure through which the objectives of the company are set, and the means of attaining those objectives and monitoring performance are determined. Good corporate governance should provide proper incentives for the board and management to pursue objectives that are in the interests of the company and shareholders and should facilitate effective monitoring, thereby encouraging firms to use resources more efficiently."

Most definitions that center on the company itself (an internal perspective) do, however, have certain elements in common, which can be summarized as follows:

Corporate governance is a system of relationships, defined by structures and processes: For example, the relationship between shareholders and management consists of the former providing capital to the latter to achieve a return on their (shareholder) investment. Managers in turn are to provide shareholders with financial and operational reports on a regular basis and in a transparent manner. Shareholders also elect a supervisory body, often referred to as the Board of Directors or Supervisory Board, to represent their interests. This body essentially provides strategic direction to and control over the company's managers. Managers are accountable to this supervisory body, which in turn is accountable to shareholders through the General Meeting of Shareholders (GMS). The structures and processes that define these relationships typically center on various performances management and reporting mechanisms.

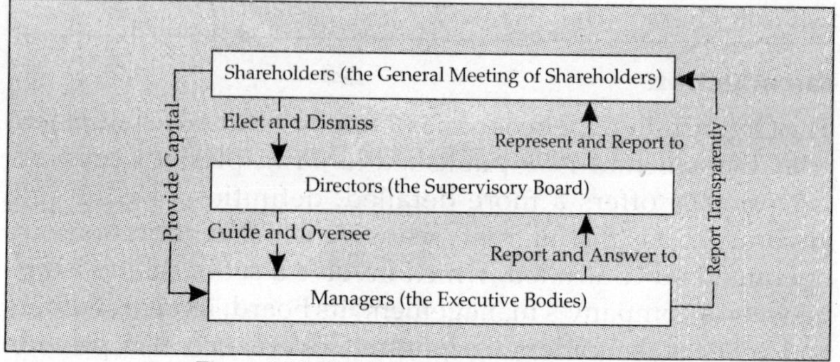

Figure 10.1: Corporate Governance System

Source: IFC, March 2

In recent years interest in corporate governance has exploded. There are a number of reasons for this but perhaps the most important is the corporate governance scandals that have occurred in the US, Europe, and elsewhere. But what exactly is corporate governance? One common way of using the term is based on the following narrow definition. This is how the term is typically used in Anglo-Saxon countries such as the US and UK. The standard mechanisms for ensuring that this occurs are *(i)* the board of directors; *(ii)* executive compensation; *(iii)* the market for corporate control; *(iv)* concentrated holdings and monitoring by financial institutions; and *(v)* debt. Underlying this narrow view of corporate governance is Adam Smith's notion of the invisible hand as the key principle that the organization of the economy is based on. Corporate governance reform has emerged as a critical business issue, thrust on the world stage by a number of high profile corporate failures. While many regulatory efforts are underway to identify and codify good governance practices to rebuild public and market trust, there are a parallel number of efforts to map out the social and environmental—non-financial—boundaries of corporate governance. The purpose of this study is to probe these issues further. What is the degree and nature of convergence of social, environmental and governance practices of corporations? What are the governance practices that exemplify the best practice of social and environmental performance and how fundamental are these governance practices to a company's effective financial and non financial performance? What are the factors driving these trends and will the social and environmental aspects of corporate governance grow in importance in the future?

Why is Corporate Governance Important?

Corporate governance refers to the way that Boards oversee the running of a company by its managers, and how Board members are held accountable to shareowners and the company. This has implications for company behavior not only to shareowners but also to employees, customers, those financing the company, and other stakeholders, including the communities in which the business operates. Research shows that responsible management of environmental, social and governance issues creates a business ethos and environment that builds both company's integrity within society and the trust of its shareowners.

Principles for Corporate Governance

Corporate governance is only part of the larger economic context in which firms operate, which includes, for example, macroeconomic policies and the degree of competition in product and factor markets. The corporate governance framework also depends on the legal, regulatory, and institutional environment. In addition, factors such as business ethics and corporate awareness of the environmental and societal interests of the communities in which it operates can also have an impact on the reputation and the long-term success of a company. OECD have assembled a system of principles that are intended to assist member and non-member governments in their efforts to evaluate and improve the legal, institutional and regulatory framework for corporate governance in their countries, and to provide guidance and suggestions for stock exchanges, investors, corporations, and other parties that have a role in the process of developing good corporate governance.

The basic principles for corporate governance are:

1. Oversight and management of risk.
2. Oversight of the preparation of the entity's financial statements.
3. Principles on the other hand is a form of self-regulation. It allows the sector to determine what standards are acceptable or unacceptable. It also pre-empts overzealous legislations that might not be practical.

Business Ethics Turns Crime Severity of Corporate Governance

Business ethics can be both a normative and a descriptive discipline. As a corporate practice and a career specialization, the field is primarily normative. In academia descriptive approaches are also taken. The range and quantity of business ethical issues reflects the degree to which business is perceived to be at odds with non-economic social values. Firms and corporations operate in the social and natural environment. By virtue of existing in the social and natural environment, business is duty bound to be accountable to the natural and social environment in which it survives.

General Ethics in Business

1. Issues regarding the moral rights and duties between a company and its shareholders: fiduciary responsibility, stakeholder concept *vs*. shareholder concept.
2. Irrespective of the demands and pressures upon it, business by virtue of its existence is bound to be ethical.

As an academic discipline, business ethics emerged in the 1970s. Since no academic business ethics journals or conferences existed, researchers published their papers in general management outlets, and attended general conferences, such as the Academy of Management. Over time, several peer-reviewed journals appeared, and more researchers entered the field. Especially, higher interest in business topics among academics was observed after several corporate scandals in the earlier 2000s.

International Scope of Corporate Governance

Numerous codes of best practices and corporate governance principles have been developed over the last ten years. Worldwide, over 100 codes have been written in some 40 countries and regions. Most of these codes focus on the role of the Supervisory Board (or Board of Directors) in the company. A handful are international in scope. Among these, only the OECD principles address both policy makers and businesses, and focus on the entire governance framework (shareholder rights, stakeholders, disclosure, and board practices). The OECD principles have gained worldwide acceptance as a framework and reference point for corporate governance. Published in 1999 and revised in 2004, they were developed to provide principle based guidance on good governance.

OECD Corporate Governance Framework

The OECD corporate governance framework is built on four core values:

Fairness: The corporate governance framework should protect shareholder rights and ensure the equitable treatment of all shareholders, including minority and foreign shareholders. All shareholders should have the opportunity to obtain effective redress for violations of their rights.

Responsibility: The corporate governance framework should recognize the rights of stakeholders as established by law, and encourage active co-operation between corporations and stakeholders in creating wealth, jobs, and the sustainability of financially sound enterprises.

Transparency: The corporate governance framework should ensure that timely and accurate disclosure is made on all material matters regarding the company, including its financial situation, performance, ownership, and governance structure. Timely and accurate disclosure is made on all material matters regarding the company, including its financial situation, performance, ownership, and governance structure.

Accountability: The corporate governance framework should ensure the strategic guidance of the company, the effective monitoring of management by the board, and the board's accountability to the company and shareholders.

Current Issues in Corporate Governance

Financial economists have been interested in corporate governance for much longer and for more fundamental developments that have fundamentally changed the face and nature of international capital markets and financial systems over the last twenty years:

- Privatisations;
- Growth of pension and other fund investment;
- Mergers waves and takeovers;
- Deregulation;
- European and international capital market integration.

Conclusion

This thought-leader study on the convergence between corporate governance and corporate social responsibility has been conducted during a period of great debate regarding the definition of good governance. The boundaries and definition of corporate governance are in a period of significant flux such that emergent CSR issues have made it on the radar of many companies and regulators around the world as never before. By and large the thought-leaders interviewed for their views on the convergence between corporate governance and corporate social responsibility were not a homogenous group. Their views differed fundamentally in a few areas and converged in others. To start, many of them do not use the term CSR, preferring corporate responsibility or other variations. While there was some dispute as to what was meant by convergence, they were unanimous in their view that CSR is an emergent area of risk in the broadening portfolio of risk management. No one really argued that the reclassification of risk to include the management of non-financial risks implied a convergence—though a number of interviewees advanced the view that CSR and governance are converging at the values level of governance, a result of the reclassification of the boundaries of corporate accountability to include non-financial stakeholder issues.

The function of developing and the implantation of an "ethics system" is difficult, because there is no clear, nor any singular decisive way that is able to be presented as a standard across the board for any organization—as due to each organization's own culture. Also, the implementation should be done accordingly to the entire areas of operations within the organization. If it is not implemented pragmatically and with empathic caution for the needs, desires, and personalities of the stakeholders, or the culture, then unethical views may be taken by the stakeholders, or even unethical behavior throughout the organization.

Corporate governance is a young academic field characterized by partial theories, limited access to high-quality data, inconsistent empirics, and unresolved methodological problems. Corporate governance affects the development and functioning of capital markets and exerts a strong influence on resource allocation. In an era of increasing capital mobility and globalization, it has also become an important framework condition affecting the industrial competitiveness and economies.

References

1. "Value at Risk: Climate Change and the Future of Governance" CERES Sustainable Governance Project Report, April 2002, Innovest Strategic Value Advisors, Coalition for Environmentally Responsible Economies, Boston.
2. Ellul, Andrew, Levent Guntay, and Ugur Lel, 2006, "External Governance and Debt Agency Costs of Family Firms," Available at SSRN: http://ssrn.com/abstract=687371.
3. Khanna, Tarun, Joe Kogan, and Krishna Palepu, 2006, "Globalization and Similarities in Corporate Governance: A Cross-Country Analysis," *The Review of Economics and Statistics* 88(1), pp.69-90.
4. Switzer, Lorne N. and Catherine Kelly "Corporate governance mechanisms and the performance of small-cap firms in Canada", *International Journal of Business Governance and Ethics,* 2006 - Vol. 2, No.3/4.
5. Bainbridge, S. (2008), *The New Corporate Governance in Theory and Practice*, New York : Oxford University Press.
6. Sun, William (2009), *How to Govern Corporations So They Serve the Public Good: A Theory of Corporate Governance Emergence*, New York: Edwin Mellen.
7. Özekmekçi, Abdullah, Mert (2004), *The Correlation between Corporate Governance and Public Relations*, Istanbul Bilgi University.
8. Monks, Robert A.G. and Minow, Nell, *Corporate Governance*, Blackwell, 2004, ISBN.

Corporate Governance in India
An overview

Prof. Suresh Vadde
Prof. Ch. Srikanthverma

ABSTRACT

The focus on corporate governance has grown exponentially over the last decade. The concept of corporate governance, which emerged as a response to corporate failures and widespread dissatisfaction with the way many corporate function, has become one of the wide and deep discussions across the globe recently. It primarily hinges on complete transparency, integrity and accountability of the management. There is also an increasingly greater focus on investor protection and public interest. Corporate governance is concerned with the values, vision and visibility. It is about the value orientation of the organization, ethical norms for its performance, the direction of development and social accomplishment of the organization and the visibility of its performance and practices. Corporate governance is the system by which companies are directed and managed. It influences how the objectives of the company are set and achieved, how risk is monitored and assessed and how performance is optimized. Sound corporate governance is therefore critical to enhance and retain investors' trust. This paper looks at some of the different definitions of corporate governance as well as the importance of corporate governance. It then goes on to discuss pre-liberalization, post-liberalization and the current state of corporate governance in India. It also highlights the mechanisms and control, principles and problems of corporate governance.

Introduction

Corporate governance is the set of processes, customs, policies, laws, and institutions affecting the way a corporation (or company) is directed, administered or controlled. Corporate governance also includes the relationships among the many stakeholder involved and the goals for which the corporation is governed. The principal stakeholders are the shareholders, the board of directors, employees, customers, creditors, suppliers, and the community at large. Corporate governance is a multi-faceted subject. An important theme of corporate governance is to ensure the accountability of certain individuals in an organization through mechanisms that try to reduce or eliminate the principal-agent problem. A related but separate thread of discussions focuses on the impact of a corporate governance system in economic efficiency, with a strong emphasis on shareholders' welfare. There are yet other aspects to the corporate governance subject, such as the stakeholder view and the corporate governance models around the world. There has been renewed interest in the corporate governance practices of modern corporations since 2001, particularly due to the high-profile collapses of a number of large U.S. firms such as Enron Corporation and MCI Inc. (formerly WorldCom). In 2002, the U.S. federal government passed the Sarbanes-Oxley Act, intending to restore public confidence in corporate governance.

While the term corporate governance has been widely used, it has not been clearly defined. In general, corporate governance is viewed as a system by which business corporations are directed and controlled. The corporate governance structure specifies the distribution of rights and responsibilities among different participants in the corporation, such as, the board, managers, shareholders and other stakeholders, and spells out the rules and procedures for making decisions on corporate affairs. In this paper, we define corporate governance as "a set of relationships between a company's management, its board, its shareholders and other stakeholders. Corporate governance also provides the structure through which the company objectives are set and the means of attaining those objectives and monitoring performance".

Definition

The providers of finance to corporations be it individuals, mutual/pension funds, banks, financial institutions or even governments require assurances that their investments are both productive and protected. Effective corporate governance is about providing those assurances. According to Millstein (1998), the term corporate governance can be defined both narrowly as well as more broadly.

Millstein (1998), in the narrow version of her definition, describes corporate governance as the relationship between managers, directors and shareholders. This narrow definition encompasses also the relationship of the corporation to stakeholders and society. Whereas in the broader version of her definition, corporate governance encompasses the combination of laws, regulations, listing rules and voluntary private sector practices that enable the corporation to attract capital, perform efficiently, generate profit and meet both legal obligations as well as the expectations of society generally. Furthermore, she states that no matter what the definition, basically corporate governance concerns the means by which a corporation assures investors that it has in place well performing management who ensure that corporate assets provided by investors are being put to appropriate and profitable use.

Millstein (1998) further found, when looking at the question of 'for whom the corporation was governed', a number of different models of corporate governance. Some nations, in particular the continental Europeans focus on the need to satisfy societal expectations in particular the interests of other "stakeholders", defined to include suppliers, creditors, tax authorities as well as local communities. Whereas others mostly the Anglo-Saxon countries gave precedence to the primacy of ownership and property rights and focus the corporate objective on returning a profit to shareholders over the longer term.

In addition, the report issued in 1998 by the OECD Business Sector Advisory Group on Corporate Governance which was chaired by Millstein [henceforth called the Millstein Report (1998)] found that maximizing long-term shareholder value encourages investment capital to be put to the most efficient economic use and this benefits society.

The Millstein Report (1998) goes on to add however that stakeholder and shareholder interests are not necessarily mutually exclusive. She observes that corporations do not succeed by consistently neglecting the expectations of the other stakeholders but at the same time neither can they attract much needed capital from the equity markets if they fail to meet shareholders' expectations of a competitive return. Hence the most successful corporations from the corporate governance perspective are those that are able to strike the right balance between the interests of shareholders and the interests of the other stakeholders.

Importance

As a result of globalization and the increasing complexity of business there is a greater reliance on the private sector as the engine of growth in both developed and developing countries. Corporations are legal entities created by societies because they are an efficient form of organization and society benefits from their existence. Corporations contribute to economic growth and development, which in turn leads to improve the standards of living as well as alleviation of poverty. The end result of all this activity is the creation of more stable political systems. Furthermore as noted by Gregory and Simms (1999), the quality of corporate governance is important since it has a direct impact on the efficiency with which a corporation employs assets; its ability to attract low-cost capital; its ability to meet the expectations of society and overall performance of corporation.

Efficiency with which a corporation employs assets

Effective corporate governance ensures the optimal use of resources both intra-firm and inter-firm. With effective systems of corporate governance, debt and equity capital will go to those corporations capable of investing it in the most efficient manner for the production both of highly demanded goods and services as well as those with the highest rate of return. This helps to protect and nurture scarce resources thereby ensuring that societal needs are met. In all probability this will mean that incompetent managers are replaced. These efficiency effects both as to scarce resources and the quality of managers should apply whether a firm is a state owned enterprise, a private closely held firm owned by a family group, or a publicly traded corporation on a stock exchange.

Ability to attract low-cost capital

Effective corporate governance also helps to lower the cost of capital by improving the confidence of both foreign and domestic investors that their assets will be used for the purposes agreed. A survey of institutional investors by R.F. Felton et al. (1996) found that they would willingly pay on average well over ten percentage points more for a "well-governed" company, all other things being equal. In competitive markets, this means that managers must constantly evolve new strategies to meet the changing circumstances. This requires that managers be empowered to make decisions. However, as observed by that famous 18th century economist Adam Smith, managers may have incentives to act in their own self-interest under such circumstances. Jensen and Meckling (1976) found that when firm ownership is separated from control, the manager's self- interest may lead to the misuse of corporate assets, for example through pursuit of overly risky or imprudent projects. Therefore we need to have in place rules and regulations to protect the best interests of the providers of capital. They include the following:

i. Independent monitoring of management.

ii. Transparency about the performance, ownership and control of the corporation.

iii. Participation in certain fundamental decisions by the shareholders.

Ability to meet the expectations of society

For long-term success, corporations must comply with the laws, regulations and expectations of societies where they operate. Many corporations take their role as corporate citizens seriously thus contributing to civil society. Regrettably however, some corporations are opportunistic and seek to profit from child labor or act without regard for the environment. The latter are not merely failures of corporate governance but are symptomatic of the larger failures of government to provide the framework needed to hold corporations responsible for issues that are also important for society at large.

Impact on overall performance

When corporate governance is effective, it provides managers with oversight and holds boards and managers accountable in their management of corporate assets. This oversight and accountability combined with the efficient use of resources, improved access to lower-cost capital and increased responsiveness to societal needs and expectations should lead to improved corporate performance. Effective corporate governance should make it more likely that managers focus on improving firm performance and are replaced when they fail to do so. A study carried out by Millstein and MacAvoy in the United States analyzing data from 1991-95 found that U.S. corporations with active and independent boards of directors generated higher economic profit hence supporting the reasonable assumption that corporate governance matters to corporate performance. Effective corporate governance also helps to reduce corruption in business dealings by making it difficult for corrupt practices to develop and take root in a company.

History of Corporate Covernance in India

Pre-liberalization

When India attained independence in 1947, the country was poor, with an average per-capita annual income under thirty dollars. However, it still possessed sophisticated laws regarding "listing, trading, and settlements." It even had four fully operational stock exchanges. Subsequent laws, such as the 1956 Companies Act, further solidified the rights of investors. In the decades following India's independence, the country turned away from its capitalist past and embraced socialism. The 1951 Industries Act was a step in this direction, requiring "that all industrial units obtain licenses from the central government." The 1956 Industrial Policy Resolution stipulated that "the public sector would dominate the economy." To put this plan into effect, the Indian government created enormous state-owned enterprises, and India steadily moved toward a culture of "corruption, nepotism and inefficiency." As the government took over floundering private enterprises and rejuvenated them, it essentially "converted private bankruptcy to high-cost public debt." One scholar referred to India's economic history as "the institutio-nalization of inefficiency."

The absence of a corporate-governance framework exacerbated the situation. Government accountability was minimal, and the few private companies that remained on India's business landscape enjoyed free reign with respect to most laws; the government rarely initiated punitive action, even for non-conformity with basic governance laws. Boards of directors invariably were staffed by friends or relatives of management, and abuses by dominant shareholders and management were common place. India's equity markets "were not liquid or sophisticated enough" to punish these abuses.

Scholars believe that "takeover threats act as a disciplining mechanism to poorly performing companies" because as the stock price of poorly governed firms decreases (because disgruntled investors discard stock), the firms become susceptible to hostile-takeover attempts. Thus, "the fear of a takeover ... is supposed to keep the management honest." However, until recently, hostile takeovers were almost entirely non-existent in India, and therefore, the poorly governed Indian firms had little to worry about in terms of following corporate laws once they had raised capital through their initial public offering. Thus, corporate governance in India was in a dismal condition by the early 1990s.

Post-liberalization

In 1999, in a defining moment in India's corporate-governance history, the Indian Parliament created the Securities and Exchange Board of India (SEBI) to "protect the interests of investors in securities and to promote the development of, and to regulate the securities market." In the years leading up to 2000, as Indian enterprises turned to the stock market for capital, it became important to ensure good corporate governance industry-wide. Additionally, a plethora of scams rocked the Indian business scene, and corporate governance emerged as a solution to the problem of unscrupulous corporate behavior.

In 1998, the Confederation of Indian Industry—India's premier business association—unveiled India's first code of corporate governance. However, since the Code's adoption was voluntary, few firms embraced it. Soon after, SEBI appointed the Birla Committee to fashion a code of corporate governance. In 2000, SEBI accepted the recommendations of the Birla Committee and introduced Clause 49 into the Listing Agreement of Stock Exchanges. Clause 49 outlines requirements vis-a-vis corporate governance in exchange-traded companies. In 2003, SEBI instituted the Murthy Committee to scrutinize India's corporate-governance framework further and to make additional recommendations to enhance its effectiveness. SEBI has since incorporated the recommendations of the Murthy Committee, and the latest revisions to Clause 49 became law on January 1, 2006.

Current State of Corporate Governance in India

Corporate governance reform in India has focused primarily on the "role and composition of the board of directors." Each of the three sets of recommendations (the CII Code recommendations from 1997, the Kumar Mangalam Birla Committee recommendations from 2000, and the Murthy Committee recommendations from 2003) has advanced a more nuanced and sophisticated understanding of corporate governance in this respect. For example, while the CII Code was silent on the financial-literacy levels expected of directors, the Murthy Committee recommended that companies train their "Board members ... in the business model of the company as well as the risk profile of the business parameters of the company." Another notable recommendation of the Murthy Committee was that the Audit Committee be comprised entirely of "financially literate non-executive members with at least one member having accounting or related financial.

Corporate Governance Mechanisms and Control

Corporate governance mechanisms and controls are designed to reduce the inefficiencies that arise from moral hazard and adverse selection. For example, to monitor managers' behaviour, an independent third party (the external auditor) attests the accuracy of information provided by management to investors. An ideal control system should regulate both motivation and ability.

Internal corporate governance controls

Internal corporate governance controls monitor activities and then take corrective action to accomplish organizational goals. Examples include:

Monitoring by the board of directors: The board of directors, with its legal authority to hire, fire and compensate top management, safeguards invested capital. Regular board meetings allow potential problems to be identified, discussed and avoided. Whilst non-executive directors are thought to be more independent, they may not always result in more effective corporate governance and may not increase performance. Different board structures are optimal for different firms. Moreover, the ability of the board to monitor the firm's executives is a function of its access to information. Executive directors possess superior knowledge of the decisionmaking process and therefore evaluate top management on the basis of the quality of its decisions that lead to financial performance outcomes, exante. It could be argued, therefore, that executive directors look beyond the financial criteria.

Internal control procedures and internal auditors: Internal control procedures are policies implemented by an entity's board of directors, audit committee, management, and other personnel to provide reasonable assurance of the entity achieving its objectives related to reliable financial reporting, operating efficiency, and compliance with laws and regulations. Internal auditors are personnel within an organization who test the design and implementation of the entity's internal control procedures and the reliability of its financial reporting.

Balance of power: The simplest balance of power is very common; require that the President be a different person from the Treasurer. This application of separation of power is further developed in companies where separate divisions check and balance each other's actions. One group may propose company-wide administrative changes, another group review and can veto the changes, and a third group check that the interests of people (customers, shareholders, employees) outside the three groups are being met.

Remuneration: Performance-based remuneration is designed to relate some proportion of salary to individual performance. It may be in the form of cash or non-cash payments such as shares and share options, superannuation or other benefits. Such incentive schemes, however, are reactive in the sense that they provide no mechanism for preventing mistakes or opportunistic behaviour, and can elicit myopic behaviour.

External corporate governance controls

External corporate governance controls encompass the controls external stakeholders exercise over the organisation. Examples include:

- Competition
- Debt covenants
- Demand for and assessment of performance information (especially financial statements)
- Government regulations
- Managerial labour market
- Media pressure
- Takeovers

Principles of Corporate Governance

Key elements of good corporate governance principles include honesty, trust and integrity, openness, performance orientation, responsibility and accountability, mutual respect, and commitment to the organization. Of importance is how directors and management develop a model of governance that aligns the values of the corporate participants and then evaluate this model periodically for its effectiveness. In particular, senior executives should conduct themselves honestly and ethically, especially concerning actual or apparent conflicts of interest, and disclosure in financial reports.

Rights and equitable treatment of shareholders: Organizations should respect the rights of shareholders and help shareholders to exercise those rights. They can help shareholders exercise their rights by effectively communicating information that is understandable and accessible and encouraging shareholders to participate in general meetings.

Interests of other stakeholders: Organizations should recognize that they have legal and other obligations to all legitimate stakeholders.

Role and responsibilities of the board: The board needs a range of skills and understanding to be able to deal with various business issues and have the ability to review and challenge management performance. It needs to be of sufficient size and have an appropriate level of commitment to fulfill its responsibilities and duties. There are issues about the appropriate mix of executive and non-executive directors.

Integrity and ethical behaviour: Ethical and responsible decision making is not only important for public relations, but it is also a necessary element in risk management and avoiding lawsuits. Organizations should develop a code of conduct for their directors and executives that promotes ethical and responsible decision-making. It is important to understand, though, that reliance by a company on the integrity and ethics of individuals is bound to eventual failure. Because of this, many organizations establish Compliance and Ethics Programs to minimize the risk that the firm steps outside of ethical and legal boundaries.

Disclosure and transparency: Organizations should clarify and make publicly known the roles and responsibilities of board and management to provide shareholders with a level of accountability. They should also implement procedures to independently verify and safeguard the integrity of the company's financial reporting. Disclosure of material matters concerning the organization should be timely and balanced to ensure that all investors have access to clear, factual information.

Issues Involving in Corporate Governance

- Internal controls and internal auditors.
- The independence of the entity's external auditors and the quality of their audits.
- Oversight and management of risk.
- Oversight of the preparation of the entity's financial statements.
- Review of the compensation arrangements for the chief executive officer and other senior executives.

- The resources made available to directors in carrying out their duties.
- The way in which individuals are nominated for positions on the board.
- Dividend policy.

Problems of Corporate Governance

Demand for information: In order to influence the directors, the shareholders must combine with others to form a significant voting group which can pose a real threat of carrying resolutions or appointing directors at a general meeting.

Monitoring costs: A barrier to shareholders using good information is the cost of processing it, especially to a small shareholder. The traditional answer to this problem is the efficient market hypothesis (in finance, the efficient market hypothesis (EMH) asserts that financial markets are efficient), which suggests that the small shareholder will free ride on the judgements of larger professional investors.

Supply of accounting information: Financial accounts form a crucial link in enabling providers of finance to monitor directors. Imperfections in the financial reporting process will cause imperfections in the effectiveness of corporate governance. This should, ideally, be corrected by the working of the external auditing process.

Conclusion

There is a heightened awareness worldwide that effective corporate governance as manifested by transparency, accountability as well as the just and equitable treatment of shareholders is now a pre-requisite towards efforts to promote sustainable development. Towards this end, there is a need for both public (as represented by governments) and private sector partnership to raise the awareness of the importance of corporate governance improvements and to assist in implementing corporate governance reform. However, such efforts must be mindful of the fact that each country has its own culture as well as differing social and economic priorities. Similarly every corporation has its own corporate culture and business goals. All of these differences will impinge on questions regarding the most practical corporate governance structures and practices to be adopted both by sovereign nations and individual corporations. Therefore, at this point of time, to get a consensus on a single model of corporate governance or a single set of detailed governance rules is both unlikely and unnecessary. It is expected that over time the dictates of the capital market will lead to increasing convergence in practice between countries. This together with globalization and the attendant fall in regulatory barriers between countries will ensure that investment capital flows to those corporations that have adopted efficient corporate governance standards including internationally acceptable accounting and auditing standards; adequate investor protection mechanisms as well as board practices designed to provide independent and accountable oversight of managers.

References

1. Adam Smith, *An Inquiry into the Nature and Causes of the Wealth of Nations*, Edwin Cannan, Ed., University of Chicago Press 1976, pp. 264-265.

2. Business Sector Advisory Group Report to the OECD on "Corporate Governance:" Improving Competitiveness and Access to Capital in Global Markets, April 1998.

3. The "Millstein Report", pp. 9 and 20.

4. Felton, R.F. (1996). 'Putting a Value on Board Governance', *McKinsey Quarterly*, pp. 170-174.

5. Greenspan, A. (1999). 'Lessons from the Global Crisis', Remarks to the World Bank Group and International Monetary Fund Program of Seminars, Washington, D.C., September 27, 1999.

6. Gregory, H.J. and Simms, M.E. (1999), "Corporate Governance: What It Is and Why It Matters", Paper presented at the 9th International Anti-Corruption Conference, Durban, South Africa, October 11, 1999.

7. Harvey, C.R. and Roper, A.H. (1999), *'The Asian Bet', Financial Markets and Development*, Harwood, Litan and Pomerleano, Editors 1999, pp.29 and 144.

8. Millstein, I.M. (1998), 'The Evolution of Corporate Governance in the United States', Remarks to the World Economic Forum, Davos, Switzerland, February 2, 1998.

9. Jensen, M.C. and Meckling, W.H. (1976), "Theory of the Firm: Managerial Behavior, Agency Costs and Ownership Structure", *Journal of Financial Economics*, pp. 305-309.

10. Millstein, I.M.(1998), 'The Basics of a Stable Global Economy', *The Journal of Commerce*, November 30, 1998.

11. Millstein, I.M. and MacAvoy, P.W. (1998), 'The Active Board of Directors and Performance of the Large Publicly Traded Corporation', 98 *Columbia Law Review* 1283, pp. 1291-1299.

12. Wolfensohn, J.D. (1999). 'A Battle for Corporate Honesty', *The Economist: The World in 1999*, pp. 38.

Business Ethics and Corporate Governance

G. Jayakar Rao

ABSTRACT

Business corporations are increasingly important for wealth creation and how companies are operated will influence society as whole. To serve this wealth creation function, companies must focus on their objectives and be accountable for their actions through the structure of good corporate governance.

Corporate governance as Business Ethics issue is a hundred times more powerful than internet and globalization and can destroy businesses in a very short span of time. To impress public the corporate governance are changing rapidly losing standards. In Business what was considered bad is now good and what is good is becoming bad. Standards for corporate governance that have worked for decades are looking old fashioned and immoral.

An attempt to bring back the way businesses have to be and the way to have right business perceptions with the help of Ethics. The changes that are taking place in the corporate governance today depicts that the companies are more interested in the long-term sustainability than a short term. The attempt is to make sure that the changing trend of Business Ethics in the global scenario of corporate governance has advantages as well as disadvantages. The failure in corporate governance has forced companies to think in the right direction of right ways.

CORPORATE GOVERNANCE

"The internal means by which corporations are operated and controlled, which involve a set of relationships between a company's management, its board, its shareholders and other stakeholders is called as corporate governance.

Corporate governance also provides the structure through which the objectives of the company are set, and the means of attaining those objectives and monitoring performance are determined. Good corporate governance should provide proper incentives for the board and management to pursue objectives that are in the interests of the company and shareholders, and should facilitate effective monitoring; thereby encouraging firms to use resources more efficiently."[1]

If we consider the qualities of a successful firm then it is imperative to understand that the foremost and the fundamental will be - to meet the needs of the market. To understand what the market needs may vary as the market segmentation plays a very important role. If the market demands for socially responsible behavior then we know that firms will be successful only when it demonstrates the same.

According to a study, (*Business Week Review*) in Americas out of 1000 America it was found that 95 per cent rejected the notion that a firm's role is limited to Profit Maximization. I am sure the same would be the condition in the Indian perspective as well. Further to this study it is understood that a firm which treats their employees well is proved to have more loyal, effective and productive employees.

If we consider a situation, where the market does not demand a socially responsible firm then it is a question to the firm to behave socially responsible or not. There are many arguments regarding the firm's responsibility. To employees? To Society? To Stakeholders? To Consumers? It is clear that it is not possible for any Firm to satisfy each and everything. There is a fair good chance for firms to focus on profit maximization as it will surely serve the purpose of sharing the same profits to their stakeholders.

There is a link between ethics and corporate governance. Companies and individuals are concerned. Ethics is to do more than what you are legally required to do in order to fulfill your legal obligations. Drivers, leadership have to lead companies to do better.

The definition of Business Ethics is the application of ethical values to business behavior. It deals with openness, responsibility and integrity. The main question is how the company does its business.

The code and its message have to be circulated within the company. Training must be organized to create a consistency of conduct within the business so that everyone will know how to face a critical dilemma and what they are expected. The company culture should set the tone of the attitudes.

As early as 1970 American Businesses argued that the firm's social responsibility as primarily to its stakeholders and therefore the main objective of the firm is to earn profits.

There are some more ways to understand the values and ethics in businesses that at any given point of time the person who starts the business would set aside personal ethics and values in order to meet the needs of the firm. But it will be a wrong perception to think of a situation where a person has to leave his personal ethics before he enters into his corporate world.

"The virtue of ethical decision we make is based on a set of dispositions we have acquired throughout our life. When someone acts unethically in a business transaction, this is bound to break down the good character habit that he or she has developed up to this point. The virtue theorist denies that there is an ability to separate the 'business' self from the 'private' self, because the actions in each realm form disposition which apply to person's general manner of acting".[2]

The influence that a business has on an individual and the community has to be placed on a moral base than on any other thing. As morals are integral to a community or a society the need base for a business has to be in the same lines.

A great example of ethical behavior is depicted by Johnson and Johnson company. The way it handles critical ethical decisions demonstrate that the priority it has for consumers stands in first place and second is its employees and third its management and fourth is to communities and fifth and last is to its stockholders. Few instances have shown that the Johnson and Johnson has cut down their profit by more than 50 per cent as they recalled their products from the markets.

We also have an example of Satyam Computers which has depicted its priorities in a different way. The statement made by Mr. Ramalinga Raju in January 2009 has not only devastated many dreams of shareholders but also known to have had great impact on Sensex which hit the years lowest to 9514. It is evident that the founder (NYSE listed) of the company lacked ethics while doing business. Though it is treated as one of the biggest scams in the country but I feel that it is mere lack of Business Ethics.

BUSINESS ETHICS

Business ethics is the branch of ethics that examines ethical rules and principles within a commercial context; the various moral or ethical problems that can arise in a business setting; and any special duties or obligations that apply to persons who are engaged in commerce.

Education and Ethics

During the 32nd UNESCO General Conference (2003), Member States expressed the need to initiate and support teaching programs in ethics, not only in bioethics but in all scientific and professional education. On the basis of these recommendations and statements, UNESCO initiated the Ethics Education Programme in 2004.

The overall objective of UNESCO activities in this programme is to reinforce and increase the capacities of member states in the area of ethics education. This is a long-term objective. For the biennium 2004-2005 the activities in the area of ethics teaching have primarily focused on East and Central Europe. During 2006-2007 priority has been given to South-East Europe and part of the Arab region (Gulf region).[3]

I feel that the need of ethics education in the corporate world is needed as we observe that many corporate leaders have either emerged because of need or opportunity but very few are trained with the perspective of Business Ethics.

A consistent mode of ethics has to be maintained in the Corporates as the kind of behavior exhibited by them has an impact on the resources within. Their needs be an equation to be prepared between Business and Business Ethics. A framework needs be prepared in order to bring about Ethics in Businesses. This is possible only when persons who lead the Corporates are educated and trained. All the employees in the company are directed by Profit Maximization principle and are expected to conform to its demand. There are Corporates which have designed their own Code of Ethics and according to a study out of 90 per cent of these corporates only 28 per cent are successful in training.[4]

When numbers become more important than anything else, everything and everyone are valued in terms of a mathematical or numerical term. Employees, Values, Employees themselves and their Self identity are all inter-connected with Business Ethics. The relationship between Values and Business are like a person and God. The relationship with values is continuous one as it is lifelong process of learning but Alas. The relationships today in the world are more economic.

All the CEOs of companies should be sent to B schools to learn and understand the need of Business Ethics. This attempt will establish a new World of Corporate which will ensure that consumers and stakeholders, whom they care for, will be safe and profited.

The people who govern businesses should possess skills to promote Ethics through their exemplary life and discussions within the company.

Ethics did not emerge from Business but from Religion and Beliefs and there should be attempts made in order to train and learn the Ethics in Business.

Acquiring knowledge and educating oneself will bring civilization but not by working in a Corporate World.

We have examples of companies like Infosys which was founded by an IITan Mr. Narayana Murthy and also Satyam Mahindra by Mr. Ramalinga Raju who had attended a course in owner/president in Harvard. Both have been awarded as Entrepreneurs of the Year, but we know the present, where they individually stand. Sometimes it is disappointing, but the Corporate World takes it as a Learning Lesson and as Case Study in order to govern.

Opportunity Costs

The inclusion of Opportunity Costs into Profit Maximization is perspective that needs be understood as it considers the aspect of decision-making which revolves around people in the organization who in turn are ethically bound.

Indeed, ethics does not prevent a company from being competitive. Ethics is not against creativity and competency. The large demand from various stakeholders for ethics will bring it out in the long run as an important competitive advantage. Avoiding short-sightedness and considering the whole strategy of companies on a long term shall replace ethics at the centre of companies' considerations. There is a link between well-governed companies, long-term performance, and reduced cost of capital and equity risk. It is clear that the interests of the different stakeholders of a company converge when ethics is applied. Ethics should be then seen as an opportunity rather than a problem. Assuming that a Business has opportunity costs then the concept of Scarce Resources comes into effect as the impact directly linked or connected to efficiency. Wastage, Abuse and Misuse of these scarce resources are the results of inefficiency. Measuring its actual use with respect to its potential use provides an indication of the value of a given resource.

Good example for this could be considering the fact of the depletion of Ozone Layer and Going Green are today's concerns by many companies have their CSRs intact to handle this area. To this effect companies are squared to produce products which are environment friendly. An opportunity cost encourages the concept of consideration, it means that it considers the fact that everything and anything that possibly affect Profits should be safeguarded and especially the misuse of scarce resources or wastage would be a ground for unethical behavior.

Power *vs.* Ethics

Right use of power and influence is the Heart of Ethics—rightly been said, one of the most crucial needs of our time and one of the greatest challenges we face in leadership and in personal development. As we know that the right use of power is the crucial and an integral part of Ethics and especially considering the corporates the term power or power is often misunderstood and misused.

No one can be perfect in every decision and action but the quality of a leader in terms of his/her values, beliefs and character influences people who follow or the people whom they lead. The good character and leaders with values is more regarded as a driving force for implementing Ethics. The wise usage of Power will lead to desired results but any unwise usage will lead to unwarranted and unwanted issues.

"Leaders are expected to engage followers not just by directing them, as they are the models and mentors not martinets".[5]

Effective leadership builds but does not destroy. In Businesses we observe different types of powers being used and if the power is misused it leaves an impact on the employees, community and in turn on the image of the company. Any ethical move by a leader will appreciated and will retain people, as people just don't work for salaries—they work for more importantly for belongingness.

Through their conduct leaders (Managers) should build and create an environment where employees can work in happiness.

Approaches

Ethics and compliance can be designed with very different goals and orientations. A research has referred to two types of approaches:

(a) A compliance-based approach and

(b) An integrity or values-based approach.[6]

According to *Harvard Business Review*, a compliance based approach focuses primarily on preventing, detecting, and punishing violations of the law, while value based approach aims to define organizational values and encourage employee commitment to ethical aspirations. I feel that a value-based approach will be more effective than the compliance-based approach as it focuses on personal self governance and definitely motivates the employees to behave in accordance with shared values. In contrast compliance based approach recommends avoiding punishment instead of self governance.

The same self-governance will lead to be the base for corporate governance as well. In corporate governance we see that compliance-based approach is considered more as it safeguards the interests of external stakeholders like customers, suppliers etc.

Corporate governance should create an Ethical Climate or Culture. The elements of this culture should contain Ethical leadership, Reward system, Fairness, employee authority structure and effective communication care for employees and the community.

"Corporate governance is concerned with holding the balance between economic and social goals and between individual and communal goals. The corporate governance framework is there to encourage the efficient use of resources and equally to require accountability for the stewardship of those resources. The aim is to align as nearly as possible the interests of individuals, corporations and society." [3]

There is no single model for corporate governance. Corporate governance is a set of principles that may be variously applied in particular circumstances by government, regulators, institutions and corporations. Principles primarily designed to promote confidence in capital markets, but also have general application.

Good corporate governance is important on a number of different levels. At the company level, well-governed companies tend to have better and cheaper access to capital, and tend to out-perform their poorly governed peers over the long-term. Companies that insist upon the highest standards of governance reduce many of the risks inherent to an investment in a company. Companies that actively promote robust corporate governance practices need key employees who are willing and able to devise and implement good corporate governance policies. The companies will generally value and compensate such employees more than those of their competitors who are unaware of, or ignore, the benefits of these policies and practices. Such companies, in turn, tend to attract more investors who are willing to provide capital at lower cost.

"More generally, well-governed companies are better contributors to the national economy and society. They tend to be healthier companies that add more value to shareholders, workers, communities, and countries in contrast with poorly governed companies that may cause job and pension losses, and even undermine confidence in securities markets." [6]

Business ethicsi are usually less concerned with the foundations of ethics, or with justifying the most basic ethical principles, and are more concerned with practical problems and applications, and any specific duties that might apply to business relationships.

Employees have to determine if an act or an idea is ethical with regards to the multiplicity of situations and with the multiplicity of objectives. In a company, if diversity in values and interests is an enduring reality, it is important to establish an optimal governance process that allows different values and interests to be taken into account and to be balanced. This is the only way to find a common ethics amongst the ethics of shareholders, the ethics of Managers, and so on.

Before being a collective interest, ethics is strictly part of individuals. Everyone has his own values. Ethics is closely linked with integrity. High-level human output should therefore be considered with strong interest. Directors should be chosen with regards to their integrity, responsibility and transparency. Corporate governance like ethics is evolutionary and must be updated. Good corporate governance will enable directors to balance rightly the different views of ethics from the different stakeholders.

LINK BETWEEN BUSINESS ETHICS AND CORPORATE GOVERNANCE

"Concerning corporate governance, the first statement in 1992 from the Committee on the Financial Aspects of Corporate Governance (Cadbury Report), it is important that all employees should know what standards of conduct are expected of them. We regard it as good practice for boards of directors to draw up codes of ethics or statements of business practice and to publish them both internally and externally. Prior to 1992, less than 50 per cent of the major UK quoted companies have a code of ethics. Today almost the full one hundred have a code." [7]

There are quite many challenges which are to be considered while linking business ethics and corporate governance. As Business incorporates all the disciplines of marketing, human resources, economics, finance and accountancy, the issue like globalization and technology are the most dynamic ones. As a result to be competent and balance the ethical behavior with governance, companies have to strike a balance between all the disciplines, when this is done, the top management and the employees may also have to strike balance between their personal and professional life. Though many of them will be influenced by the circumstances, political pressure and religious stands, the ethical conduct has to RIGHT. The ethical decisions taken can be said to be decisions that ensure the safety of a society or community.

In businesses the decision-making opportunity is magnified due to the competing demands to keep business going. Some companies have implemented business ethics in their businesses and have been successful in attracting the interests of investors as well as appealed many employees.

Examples

Code of Business Conduct and Ethics (The COBE)

This Code applies to all employees of Dr. Reddy's Laboratories Ltd., its subsidiaries and affiliates (henceforth referred to as "Dr. Reddy's"). It also applies to the members of the Board of Directors in carrying out their duties as directors. It is intended as an overview of Dr. Reddy's guiding principles and is not a restatement of Dr. Reddy's policies and procedures. This Code is intended to comply with the provisions of the Sarbanes-Oxley Act of 2002 and its implementing regulations. This Code cannot and is not intended to cover every applicable law or provide answers to all questions that might arise; for that we must ultimately rely on each person's good sense of what is right, including a sense of when it is proper to seek guidance from others on the appropriate course of conduct. This Code is a general statement of goals and expectations for individual and business conduct. It is not intended to and does not in any way constitute an employment contract or assurance of continued employment, and does not create any legal rights in any employee, client, supplier, competitor, shareholder or any other person or entity.

Source: http://www.drreddys.com/media/pdf/cobe_booklet_ 2008.pdf

The Purpose and Scope of COBE of Novell

Among Novell's most fundamental operating principles are adherence to high ethical standards and compliance with all laws and regulations applicable to our business. The reputation of our Company, the quality of our work-place experience, and the satisfaction of our obligations to shareholders depend on each employee achieving these levels of conduct. The Novell Board of Directors has adopted this Code of Business Ethics (COBE) to inform all employees, including officers, of their legal and ethical obligations to Novell.

Source: http://www.novell.com/company/ir/cg/cobe/cobe.html

Conclusion

As rightly been said:

"There are those who will tell you that business and ethics cannot stand together. In the short run it might appear that companies pay a price for adhering to values while their competitors get ahead in a shorter time frame, but in the long run people would learn to distinguish, stakeholders learn to ask the right questions, and distinguish between the grain and chaff. Those that don't subscribe to values will fall by the way side; those that subscribe to values will last the course and will set benchmarks."

M. DAMODARAN,
Chairman,
Securities and Exchange Board of India.

The link between ethics and governance demonstrates that what you are doing more than what you have to do and what you are doing that should demonstrate right attitude, tone, leadership and examples. If you do not get the right attitude, governance would become a tick boxes exercise and in a long term it is not sustainable.

References

1. *Corporate Governance: Reforms* by Darryl Reed.
2. John Morse-*Journal of Applied Philosophy*.
3. www.UNESCO.org.
4. Reference book: *Perspective of Business Ethics*, Laura Hartman.
5. *Power without Morality is no longer Power*, James Baldwin (Novel).
6. L.S. Paine "Managing for Organizational integrity"- www.hbr.org
7. Philippa Foster Back, Director of the Institute of Business Ethics.

Practices of Corporate Social Responsibility of Banking Sector in India

An assessment

Sanjay Kanti Das

ABSTRACT

Corporate Social Responsibility (CSR), also known as corporate responsibility, corporate citizenship, responsible business, sustainable responsible business or corporate social performance, whatever the name means a form of corporate self regulation integrated into a business model. At present, the world over, there is an increasing awareness about Corporate Social Responsibility (CSR), Sustainable Development (SD) and Non-Financial Reporting (NFR). The contribution of financial institutions including banks to sustainable development is paramount, considering the crucial role they play in financing the economic and developmental activities of the world.

CSR developed very slowly in India though it was started a long time ago. CSR has been assuming greater importance in the corporate world, including the banking sector. There is a visible trend in the financial sector of promoting environment-friendly and socially responsible lending and investment practices.

The Government of India also pursuing the matter relating to CSR and also drafted guidelines for CSR practices time to time, namely the Guidelines issued by the Department of Public Enterprises (DPE) in November 1994, R.B.I Guidelines in Dec.2007 and Ministry of Corporate Affairs Voluntary Guidelines on CSR, 2009.

In this paper there are two separate sections. The first section covers the concept of CSR, CSR scenario in India—growth and status, while the section two covers the CSR practices in Indian banking and financial institutions, different case studies and key findings of the study and a few conclusions.

The present study is based on the case study method and an effort is made in the present study to know the status of CSR and strategies adopted for CSR in the Banking sector. Eleven banking and financial institutions are selected under stratified random sampling method from the vast network of banking and financial institutions of the country. Data are collected from the secondary sources, most particularly from concerned Banks Annual Report, web sites, newsletters and other secondary sources. The study covers the time period 2007 to 2010. From the case study, it is observed that all the financial and banking institutions of the country are directly engaged in social banking and developing banking approach. Further, all banking and financial institutions under study undertakes both fund based and non-fund based activities as a part of CSR activity. It is concluded that for the Indian banking company whatever the CSR activities are happening are centered on education, rural upliftment and helping the physically challenged. In fine, there is a need to promote a drive in banking companies towards greater accountability on CSR. In order to attain the social objectives, there is a need for framing a CSR Policy in every banking company for prioritization of activities for social spending and allocation of separate funds for this purpose.

Introduction

At present, the world over, there is an increasing awareness about Corporate Social Responsibility (CSR), Sustainable Development (SD) and Non-Financial Reporting (NFR). Consequently, there is a concerted effort among all types of organizations, to ensure that sustainable development is not lost sight of, in the pursuit of their respective goals—profit making, social service, philanthropy, etc. CSR entails the integration of social and environmental concerns by companies in their business operations as also in interactions with their stakeholders.

The contribution of financial institutions including banks to sustainable development is paramount, considering the crucial role they play in financing the economic and developmental activities of the world. In this context, the urgency for banks to act as responsible corporate citizens in the society, especially in a developing country like India need to be hardly over emphasized. Their activities should reflect their concern for human rights and environment.

Global warming and climate change are particularly important in the context of sustainable development, especially for developing countries, which tend to be ill-equipped for such changes. Therefore, all concerned shall come forward to check the situation.

Reserve Bank of India feels that, there is general lack of adequate awareness on the issue in India. In this context, the need for sustainable developmental efforts by financial institutions in India assumes urgency and banks, in particular, can help contribute to this effort by playing a meaningful role. RBI in its notification dated 20th December 2007[1] has advised banks to take note of the issues raised and consider using the same to put in place a suitable and appropriate plan of action towards helping the cause of sustainable development, with the approval of their Boards.

CORPORATE SOCIAL RESPONSIBILITY

Search for Suitable Definition

Social responsibility is the responsibility of an organisation for the impacts of its decisions and activities on society and the environment, through transparent and ethical behaviors that is consistent with sustainable development and the welfare of society and takes into account the expectations of stakeholders.

CSR is one of the effective tools that synergizes the efforts of corporate and the social sector agencies towards sustainable growth and development of social objectives at large. CSR is at heart a process of managing the costs and benefits of business activity to both internal (employees, shareholders, investors) and external (institution of public governance, community members, civil society groups, other enterprises) stakeholders.

Giving a universal definition of CSR is bit difficult as there is no common definition as such. However, there are few common threads that connect all the perspectives of CSR with each other; the dedication to serve the society being most important of them.

World Business Council for Sustainable Development (1999[2]) defines CSR as "The continuing commitment by business to behave ethically and contribute to economic development while improving the quality of life of the workforce and their families as well as of the local community and society at large."

The European Commission advocates CSR as "Being socially responsible means not only fulfilling legal expectations, but also going beyond compliance and investing more into human capital, the environment and relations with stakeholders."

CSR exhorts firms to diverge from their sole aim of maximizing profits and to lay more importance on improving the economic and social standards of the community in their countries of operation. CSR can thus be simply defined as the additional commitment by businesses to improve the social and economic status of various stakeholders involved while complying with all legal and economic requirements[3].

Thus, the meaning of CSR is two fold. On one hand, it exhibits the ethical behavior that an organization exhibits towards its internal and external stakeholders (customers as well as employees). On the other hand, it denotes the responsibility of an organization towards the environment and society in which it operates.

Existing Literature on Corporate Social Responsibility

Good corporate governance includes socially responsible business practices. A socially responsible approach to business would involve attention to social and environmental concerns in addition to economic goals and encourage companies to balance financial profits, economic value addition and social good.

Literature on CSR is enriched by the researchers of developed nations. However, so many surveys and research studies were also conducted by the researchers, academicians and institutions in Indian context. A few research organisation and professional bodies had also shown similar effort to study the status of CSR, activities of CSR in the Indian corporate sector. Keeping parity with the situation Government of India also constituted committees and sub-committees, study groups to study the status of CSR and issued several recommendations, directions and guidelines for the implementation of CSR strategies.

A survey was conducted by Business Community Foundation for TERI (The Energy and Resources Institute), Europe during the year 2001-02 and reported that a large portion of giant companies were engaged in CSR activities only. The report also notes the fact of gender discrimination at workplace and poor working condition at the workplace. Some of the major findings of the study includes *(i)* Serious and committed approach to CSR is increasing its reach, but there is vast ground yet to be covered, *(ii)* Collaboration work between companies and NGOs is increasing, *(iii)* Corporate are realizing that "Good for business is good business", and *(iv)* Most interventions so far philanthropic in nature, rather than strategic.

Another Survey was conducted jointly by Confederation of Indian Industry (CII), UNDP, British Council and Price Water Coopers (PWC) in 2002, which reported that all most all the companies under the study recognize the importance of CSR and believed that the passive philanthropy was no longer sufficient. It was also reported that a significant proportion of respondents recognized CSR as the means to enhance long-term stakeholder's value. Another most important aspect of CSR, according to the report, is that it provides an opportunity to improve relationships with local communities.

According to Hopkins (2003[4]), CSR is concerned with treating the internal and external stakeholders of the firm ethically or in a socially responsible manner and the wider aim of corporate social responsibility is to create higher and higher standards of living, while preserving the profitability of the corporation, for its stakeholders. Logsdon et al. (2006[5]) mentioned an important thing about CSR that the interpretation of CSR often changes in the area of strategic management due to the fact of varying national and cultural factors. Later on Moon and Vogel (2008[6]) reinforced it saying that CSR is highly contextual and strongly depends on the country and the state of governance of that time. However, Hopkins (2003[7]) found in his study that businesses that engage in CSR typically focus on some or all of the followings:

1. *Environment:* While focusing on this, organizations look at the environmental impacts of their products and services, as well as what they do outside the business to improve the environment.
2. *Employees:* The organizations who think in this perspective, they take care of all the employees adequately focusing on workplace conditions, benefits, living wages, and training.

3. *Communities:* The organizations that care about communities, voluntarily take advance steps to improve the quality of life for employees and their families as well as for the local community and society.

4. *Regulations:* While focusing at this point, organizations respect the laws fully and often exceed them to be more socially responsible.

5. *Emergency supports:* Sometimes organizations keep plans ready to manage business crises and ensure safety for employees and surrounding communities. Besides they also take initiatives to provide support in times of emergencies such as disaster or epidemics.

CSR Importance and its Relevance Today

Though there are existing debate about the importance and relevance of CSR in corporate sector vis-a vis in banking sector, but the following two arguments minimizes the debate and supports the role of CSR in the corporate as well as banking sector of the economy.

A moral argument for CSR

While recognizing that profits are necessary for any business entity to exist, all groups in society should strive to add value and make life better. Businesses rely on the society within which they operate and could not exist in isolation. They need the infrastructure that society provides. CSR is recognition of that inter-dependence and a means of delivering on that obligation, to the mutual benefit of businesses and the societies within which they are based.

Advocates of CSR believe that, in general, the goal of any economic system should be to augment the general social welfare. In advanced economies, the purpose of business should extend beyond the maximization of efficiency and profit. Increasingly, society expects businesses to have an obligation to the society in which they are located, to the people they employ, and their customers, beyond their traditional bottom-line and narrow shareholder concerns.

CSR advocates point out that no organization exists in isolation. They believe that businesses, without exception, have an obligation to contribute as well as draw from the community, on which they rely so heavily.

An economic argument for CSR

An economic argument in favor of CSR can also be made. It is an argument of economic self-interest—that there are very real economic benefits to businesses pursuing a CSR strategy—and is designed to persuade those business managers who are not persuaded by the moral case. CSR represents a holistic approach to business. Therefore, an effective CSR policy will infuse all aspects of operations. They believe the actions corporations take today to incorporate CSR throughout the organization represent a real point of differentiation and competitive market advantage on which future success can effect.

CSR covers all aspects of a business's day-to-day operations. Everything an organization does in some way interacts with one or more of its stakeholder groups, and companies today need to build a watertight brand with respect to all stakeholders. Whether as an employer, producer, buyer, supplier, or investment, the attractiveness and success of a company today is directly linked to the strength of its brand.

Each business entity should formulate a CSR policy to guide its strategic planning and provide a roadmap for its CSR initiatives, which should be an integral part of overall business policy and aligned with its business goals[8]. The policy should be framed with the participation of various level executives and should be approved by the Board. The core elements of CSR will revolve around:

1. Care for all stakeholders
2. Ethical functioning
3. Respect for workers' rights and welfare
4. Respect for human rights
5. Respect for environment
6. Activities for social and inclusive development.

According to strategic corporate social responsibility by William B. Werther, David Chandler[9] there are three trends which are going to have importance in future. They are increasing affluence, changing social expectation, and globalization and free flow of information.

There can be few key steps[10] to implement CSR successfully:

1. Better communication between top management and organization.
2. Appoint for CSR position.
3. Good relationship with customer, supplier, stakeholder.
4. Annual CSR audit.
5. Feedback process

CSR SCENARIO IN INDIA

CSR developed very slowly in India though it was started a long time ago. The study conducted by Chahoud et al., 2007[11] revealed that CSR in India, is still characterized mainly by philanthropic and community development activities and Indian companies and stakeholders have begun to adopt some aspects of the mainstream agenda, such as the integration of CSR into their business processes and engagement in multi-stakeholder dialogues. To describe the current state and future prospects of CSR in India Sundar (2000[12]) divided the development of CSR into four phases Table 13.1 based on the country's political and economic background. Later on, Chahoud et al. (2007) reinforced him saying that different CSR practices moved on parallel with India's historical development.

Recognizing the importance of CSR, the Ministry of Corporate Affairs, Government of India, has recently (2009) brought out a set of voluntary guidelines on CSR for corporate. These CSR guidelines pertain to areas, such as, care for all stakeholders, ethical functioning, respect for workers' rights and welfare, respect for human rights, environment and social and inclusive development.

Table 13.1: Four Phases of CSR.

Phases	Key Thurst	Key Strategies
Phase I (Till 1914)	CSR motivated by charity and philanthropy	The oldest form of CSR was motivated by charity and philanthropy with direct influence from culture, religion, family tradition, and industrialization process.
Phase II (1914-1960)	CSR for India's social development	Dominated by the country's struggle for independence and influenced fundamentally by Gandhi's theory of trusteeship for consolidation and amplification of social development. Gandhi's reform programs which included activities that sought in particular the abolition of untouchability, women's empowerment and rural development
Phase III (1960-1980)	CSR under the paradigm of the "mixed economy"	The paradigm of 'mixed economy' with the emergence of legislation on labor and Environmental standards, affected the third phase of Indian CSR. This phase is also characterized by a shift from corporate self-regulation to strict legal and public regulation of business activities.
Phase IV (1980 onwards)	CSR at the interface between philanthropic and business approaches	Indian companies and stakeholders began abandoning traditional philanthropic engagement and, to some extent, integrated CSR into a coherent and sustainable business strategy, partly adopting the multi stakeholder approach.

Source: Based on survey of literature on CSR and Sundar, P., 2000, *Beyond Business: From Merchant Charity to Corporate Citizenship*, New Delhi: Tata MacGraw-Hill

Earlier, the Committee of Public Undertakings (COPU) in 1992 examined the issue relating to social obligation of Central Public Sector Enterprises and observed that "being part of the 'State', every Public Sector Enterprise has a moral responsibility to play an active role in discharging the social obligations endowed on a welfare state, subject to the financial health of the enterprise". Based on the recommendation of the COPU, Department of Public Enterprises (DPE) issued general guidelines in November 1994. These guidelines basically left it to the Board of Directors of the Public Sector Enterprises to devise socially responsible business practices in accordance with their Articles of Association, under the general guidance of their respective Administrative Ministry/ Department.

While studying the current state of CSR in India Cheung et al. (2009) commented that India's economic reforms and its rise to become an emerging market and global player has not resulted into substantial changes in its CSR approach. Contrary to various expectations that India would adopt the global CSR standards, its present CSR approach still largely retains its own characteristics adopting only some aspects of global mainstream of CSR. Furthermore, Arora and Puranik (2004) declared that Indian CSR is still in a confused state. Their study concluded that though the Indian understanding of CSR seems to be shifting from traditional philanthropy towards sustainable business. Philanthropic patterns still remain widespread in many Indian companies and community development still plays the decisive role in CSR agenda. The underlying pattern of charity and philanthropy means that entrepreneurs sporadically donate money to external stakeholders as communities and general social welfare bodies (such as schools or hospitals) without any concrete or long-term engagement.

Ahmed (2009) contributed in the same context through an empirical research, under the supervision of ASSOCHAM Research Bureau, on 300 Indian companies which are active in 26 various theme areas for their CSR initiatives. Her research, which was later on supported by the survey of Mumbai based online organization Karmayog (2009), showed that community welfare perceived to be the top priority area on the corporate sector's list with a share of 21.93 per cent out of the total 26 activities. It involves activities that focus more towards the under-privileged community that lives around the vicinity of company plants, facilitating education and health care and supporting projects that lead to employment generation. The second most sort CSR initiative followed by Indian industrialist is towards providing education and enlightening the youth of the country. The corporate sector helps in imparting education to the deprived kids in the urban areas along with the children from rural areas that do not have any access to medium of information. They provide funds that help in setting up local schools, colleges and centers for learning and education. Since, global warming is the buzz word now a-days, Indian corporate sector as responsible members of the society have initiated their efforts to preserve and save it. Thus, environment is the third most prioritized area undertaken in CSR activities. CSR projects in this area deliver solutions that are both environmental and business friendly, providing financial benefits as well as improving the firm's image as an environmentally-aware company. The fourth most popular area, that corporate sector get involves in is the health care. They offer mobile medical services with medical help along with organizing regular medical camps to eradicate diseases, creating awareness on preventive health care among others. The Indian companies are equally extending their support in the development of the rural areas. They are providing both financial and infrastructural assistance towards agriculture, animal husbandry, cottage industries by developing local skills, using local raw materials and helping create marketing outlets. Thus, it is the fifth most prioritized area under CSR initiatives is rural development. Other CSR initiatives includes projects relating to women empowerment, donations, disaster relief, children welfare, poverty eradication, blood donation, vocational training, HIV/AIDS awareness and relief work etc. A portion of the research of Ahmed (2009) also focused on areawise concentration of CSR activities in India. The result highlighted that, out of the 20 states/UTs at India, Maharashtra received maximum attention from Indian industrialists for initiating their CSR activities followed by Gujarat, Delhi, Tamilnadu, Andhra Pradesh, West Bengal, Karnataka and Rajasthan.

Section II
CSR IN INDIAN BANKING

CSR has been assuming greater importance in the corporate world, including the banking sector. There is a visible trend in the financial sector of promoting environment-friendly and socially responsible lending and investment practices. The United Nations Environment Programme (1972) advocates that the financial sector has a role to play in protecting environment while maintaining profitability of their business. The concept of 'triple bottom-line' espoused by John Elkington, encompasses social, environmental and financial accounting. Keeping these perspectives in view, the Reserve Bank of India has rightly issued 'moral suasion' policy for banks on CSR. Recently, the Ministry of Corporate Affairs has also issued voluntary CSR guidelines for Indian corporate. The Ministry of Rural Development (MORD), Government of India has come out with "Guidelines for Rural Self Employment Institutes" and accordingly instructed the banking and financial institutions of the country to follow the spirit of the directives[13].

To highlight the role of banks in CSR the RBI circulated a notice on December 20, 2007 for all the scheduled commercial banks, with title "Corporate Social Responsibility, Sustainable Development and Non-Financial Reporting—Role of Banks". Major issues discussed in the notice were regarding Corporate Social Responsibility, Sustainable Development, and Non-Financial Reporting. Briefing about the corporate social responsibility program to other member commercial banks

RBI followed many international initiatives to highlight the importance of this notice like United Nations Environment Program Finance Initiative (UNEPFI), Global Reporting Initiative (GRI), International Finance Corporation, The Equator Principles, and Declaration on Financial Institutions.

Apart from these international initiatives, RBI report also talked about other important and urgent issues regarding global warming and extent of problem, the economics of climate change, the Happy Planet Index, the Kyoto Protocol etc. and requested to implement the same earnestly and sincerely.

In the context of Indian banking sector very little systematic documentation of CSR initiatives is available so far. However, an effort is made in this paper to present detailed CSR initiatives of Indian banking sector.

Statement of the Problem and Methodology of the Study

Both the corporate sector and banking sector of the world are talking about the implementation of CSR and in India too so many corporate entities and banking institutions are also came forward to implement the same. A lot of study was made on to know the status of CSR implementation in the world and Indian corporate sector. But only a few studies were made in respect of CSR implantation in the Indian Banking sector. A modest effort is made in the present study to know the status of CSR and strategies adopted for CSR in the Banking sector.

The present study is based on the case study method. Eleven banking and financial institutions are selected under stratified random sampling method from the vast network of banking and financial institutions of the country. Further, the present study covers seven nationalized commercial banks, two private sector banks, one co-operative bank and one development bank. Data are collected from the secondary sources, most particularly from concerned Banks Annual Report, web sites, newsletters and other secondary sources. The study covers the period 2007 to 2010.

Overall Finding of the study

From the case study of all the banking and financial institutions under study, it is observed that all the financial and banking institutions of the country is directly engaged in social banking and developing banking approach. As per the instruction of the RBI, majority of its member commercial banks started new programmes on social and economic welfare of the masses, keeping parity with the guidelines.

All Banking and financial institutions under study undertakes both fund based and non-fund based activities which have been presented in the Chart 13.1.

Loans to Weaker Sections

Loans Under Government Welfare Programme

Major Findings

1. Only one financial institution i.e. SIDBI under study has published its own CSR report keeping the benchmark of internationally accepted norms of Global Reporting Initiative (G3). However, banks like PNB, SBI, BOB and BOI publishs separate segment on CSR in their Annual Report. PNB also publishes a report on CSR strategy but it was not drafted according to internationally accepted benchmark.

2. It is also observed that only two banks namely J&K Bank and Union Bank of India follow a system of prefixed budget for pursuing CSR activities i.e. one per cent of profit after tax. While SIDBI spends 19 per cent of net profit in 2008-09 on CSR activities which is a landmark in the history of CSR funding in the banking sector of the country. It is also observed from the information supplied in the Annual Report that both—PNB and SBI—spends a huge amount for pursuing CSR activities yearly but they did not have any targeted fixed amount for doing the same expenditure.

Chart 13.1: CSR activities in Banking Sector

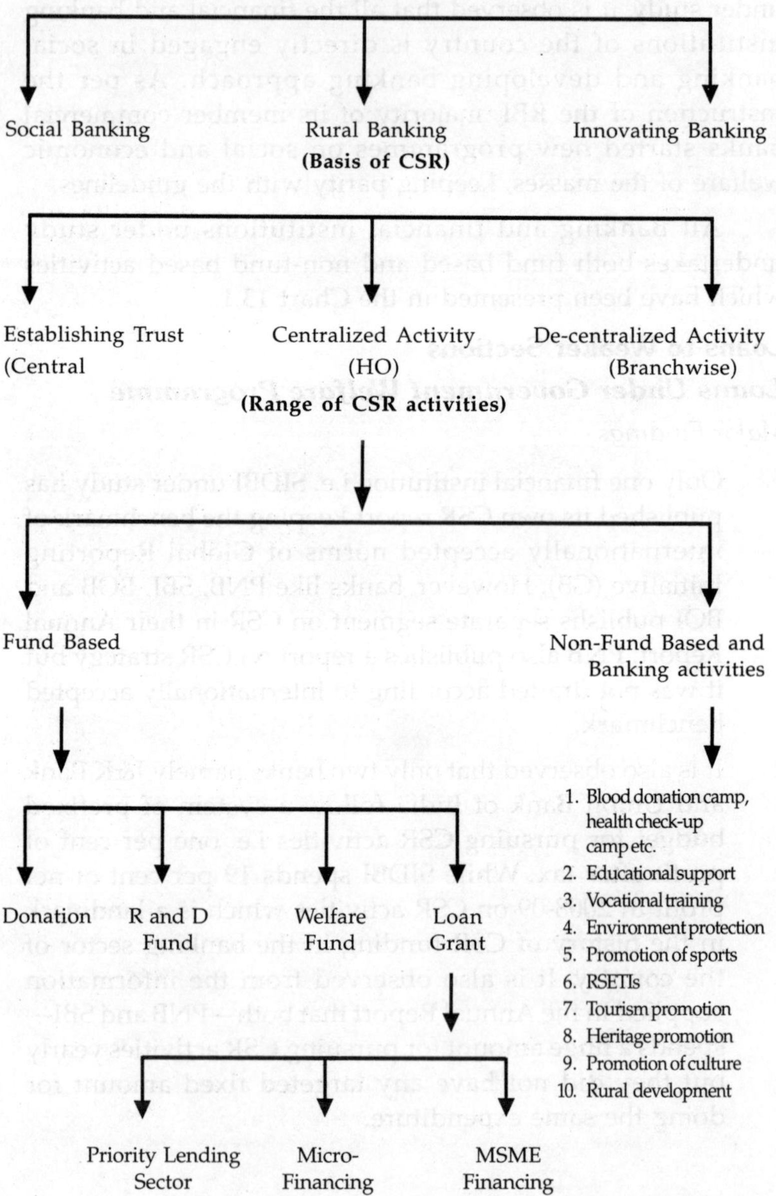

3. All most all the banks under study except J&K Bank, Ing Vysya Bank, HDFC Bank, BOI and SIDBI did not follow the Government of India (MORD) guidelines on setting up of RSETIs i.e. establishing of Rural Self Employment Institutes. BOB is the leader in the formation of RSETIs (25) followed by Allahabad Bank (21).
4. It is further observed that all the banks and financial institutions under study are engaged in spending for socio-economic development, rural development and community development projects. Further, priority sector lending, microfinancing, MSME financing and project on environment excellence etc. are common to all the financial and banking institutions.
5. It is further observed that Adoption of Girl Child by SBI, Adoption of Villages by PNB, Adoption of Orphans by Ing Vysya Bank, Heritage Preservation and Tourism Promotion by J&K Bank, Cultural Promotion by Saraswat Co-operative Bank, Retail Mobile Marketing Van for products of SHGs of Canara Bank, Rickshaw Projects of PNB etc are the unique feature of CSR activities of commercial banks in India.
6. Another significant contribution of CSR activity performed by SBI and PNB are the funding for Research and Development Grants to universities and academic institutions. The Saraswat Co-operative Bank has also promoted such activity in a different style but limited upto the state of Maharashtra.
7. Bank of India declared the fact that they forwarded over 45 per cent of net adjusted credit towards priority sector. Their CSR strategy is not as unique as they still follow the earlier social banking concepts.
8. Another feature of CSR activities which are observed from the information supplied in the annual reports by the banking companies under study is the setting up of Rural Consultancy Centre. Bank of Baroda is the leader in setting up of such consultancy centre.

Conclusion

The sad part is that CSR still has not taken off in India according to a recent survey by Mumbai based online organization "Karmayog". The second edition of the research revealed that nearly half of the top companies do nothing in the way of CSR.

For the Indian banking company whatever the CSR activities are happening are centered on education, rural upliftment and helping the physically challenged. Some of the CSR initiatives, the major banking companies have undertaken are

1. Education for all
2. Community development
3. Adoption of children
4. Vocational training
5. Rural cevelopment
6. Environment protection
7. Socio-economic development of the vulnerable sections of society.

There is a need to promote a drive in banking companies towards greater accountability on Corporate Social Responsibility (CSR). In order to attain the social objectives, there is a need for framing a CSR Policy in every banking company for prioritization of activities for social spending and allocation of separate funds for this purpose.

Moreover, to have an impact of the CSR spending and utilization of allocated budget, there should be a system of periodical monitoring and reporting to the Board of Directors.

Notes

1 "Corporate Social Responsibility, Sustainable Development and Non-Financial Reporting–Role of Banks", RBI/2007-08/ 216: DBOD No Dir. BC.58/13.27.00/20007-08, December 20, 2007.

2 World Business Council for Sustainable Development, 1999, *Corporate Social Responsibility: Meeting Changing Expectations*, World Business Council For Sustainable Development.

[3] Sandeep K. Krishnan, Rakesh Balachandran, " Corporate Social Responsibility as a determinant of market success: An exploratory analysis with special reference to MNCs in emerging markets", Marketing Strategies for Firms in Emerging Markets IIM K–NASMEI International Conference.

[4] Hopkins, Michael, 2003, *The Planetary Bargain: Corporate Social Responsibility Matters*, UK: Earthscan.

[5] Logsdon, J.M. et al., 2006, "Corporate Social Responsibility In Large Mexican Firms:, *The Journal of Corporate Citizenship*.

[6] Moon, J. and Vogel, D., 2008, *The Oxford Handbook of Corporate Social Responsibility: Corporate Social Responsibility, Government, and Civil Society In Crane*, Oxford: Oxford University Press.

[7] Ibid.

[8] Ministry of Corporate Affairs Government of India;, "Corporate Social responsibility Voluntary Guidelines", 2009.

[9] Ibid.

[10] Corporate Social Responsibility, 2003.

[11] Chahoud, Tatjana, et al., 2007, *Corporate Social and Environmental Responsibility In India—Assessing the UN Global Compac's Role*, Bonn: German Development Institute.

[12] Sundar, P., 2000, *Beyond Business: From Merchant Charity to Corporate Citizenship*, New Delhi: Tata MacGraw-Hill.

[13] The Ministry of Rural Development (MORD), Govt. of India had in the recent past conducted series of meetings of Central Level Co-ordination Committee (CLCC), the last being on 05.12.08. With a view to establish such institutes at all districts of the country, the MORD has come out with "Guidelines for Rural Self Employment Institutes (RSETIs)" on 07.01.09 covering inter alia the provision for grant assistance from Govt. of India.

References

1. Annual reports of Banking Institutions (2007-08, 2008-09, 2009-10).
2. Ahmed, Nusrat, 2009, *ASSOCHAM Eco Pulse Study: Corporate Social Responsibility 2008-09*, ASSOCHAM Research Bureau.
3. Anonymous, 2010, "More Centres For Corporate Social Responsibility Planned", Chennai: *The Hindu*.
4. Arora, B., and Puranik, R., 2004, "A Review of Corporate Social Responsibility" in India, *Journal of the Society for International Development*.

5. Barnea, Amir and Rubin, Amir, 2006, Corporate Social Responsibility as a Conflict Between Shareholders, CIBC Centre for Corporate Governance and Risk Management. http://www.sfubusiness.ca/cibc-centre. (accessed: 10/09/2010).

6. Banerjee, Subhabrata Bobby, 2007, *Corporate Social Responsibility: The Good, The Bad and The Ugly*, UK: Edward Elgar Publishing.

7. Beesley, M.E., and Evans, Tom, 1978, *Corporate Social Responsibility: A Reassessment*, Taylor and Francis.

8. Boeger, Nina, 2008, *Perspectives on Corporate Social Responsibility*, Edward Elgar Publishing.

9. Carroll, Archie B. and Buchholtz, Ann K., 2008, *Business And Society: Ethics and Stakeholder Management*, 7th Ed. USA: Cengage Learning.

10. Cheung, Yan Leung, et al., 2009, "Does Corporate Social Responsibility Matter In Asian Emerging Markets?", *Journal of Business Ethics*.

11. Crane, Andrew, Matten, Dirk, and Spence, Laura J., 2008, *Corporate Social Responsibility: Readings and cases in A global context*, Routledge.

12. Crowther, David, and Rayman-Bacchus, Lez, 2004, *Corporate Social Responsibility Series: Perspectives on Corporate Social Responsibility*, England: Ashgate Publishing, Ltd.

13. Dr. Pandey, Devendra Prasad, 2008, *Corporate Culture and Spiritual Ethic*, Allahabad: Rajiv Gandhi P.G. College.

14. Farmer, Richard N., and Hogue, Walter Dickerson. 1985, *Corporate Social Responsibility*, 2nd Ed. Lexington Books.

15. Frederick, William Crittenden, 2006, *Corporation, be Good: The Story of Corporate Social Responsibility*, United States of America: Dog Ear Publishing.

16. Friedman, M., 1962, *Capitalism And Freedom*, Chicago: University of Chicago Press.

17. Friedman, M., 1972, "Milton Friedman Responds: A Business And Society Review Interview", *Business and Society*.

18. Heal, G.M., 2008, *When Principles Pay: Corporate Social Responsibility and The Bottom Line*, Columbia University Press.

19. Hopkins, Michael, 2003, *The Planetary Bargain: Corporate Social Responsibility Matters*, UK: Earthscan.

20. Hopt, Klaus J. and Teubner, Gunther, 1985, *Corporate Governance And Directors' Liabilities: Legal, Economic, and Sociological Analyses on Corporate Social Responsibility*, Walter De Gruyter.

21. Husted, B.W. and Allen, D.B., 2007, "Corporate Social Strategy in Multinational Enterprises: Antecedents and Value Creation", *Journal Of Business Ethics*.

22. Gandhi, Mahatma Mohandas, Mohandas Gandhi Quotes. Brainy Quote, http://www.brainyquote.com/quotes/authors/m/mohand as_gandhi.html. (accessed: 25/10/2010).

23. Guthrie, J. and Parker, L., 1990, *Corporate Social Disclosure Practice: A Comparative International Analysis*, Advances in Public Interest Accounting, India Partnership Forum, 2002 National Workshop on Promoting Corporate Citizenship in India: Challenges and Opportunities. India Partnership Forum. http://www. india partnershipforum.org/resources/Background per cent20paper.pdf (accessed: 25/10/2010).

24. Jerry, W. and Rson, 1989, *Corporate Social Responsibility: Guidelines For Top Management*, Abc-Clio.

25. Kakabadse, Andrew and Morsing, Mette, 2006, *Corporate Social Responsibility: Reconciling Aspiration With Application*, Palgrave Macmillan.

26. Karmayog, 2009, "Karmayog CSR Rating 2009 of the 500 Largest Indian Companies", http://www.karmayog.org/redirect/strred.asp? docId=29464. (accessed: 25/10/2010).

27. Kotler, Philip, and Lee, Nancy, 2005, *Corporate Social Responsibility: Doing The Most Good For Your Company and Your Cause*, John Wiley and Sons.

28. Lee, Min-Dong Paul, 2008, "A Review of the Theories of Corporate Social Responsibility: Its Evolutionary Path and The Road Ahead", *International Journal of Management Reviews*.

29. Levitt, T., 1958, "The Dangers of Social Responsibility", *Harvard Business Review*.

30. Logsdon, J.M. et al., 2006, Corporate Social Responsibility in Large Mexican Firms, *The Journal of Corporate Citizenship*.

31. Lydenberg, S.D., 2005, *Corporations and the Public Interest: Guiding The Invisible Hand*, San Francisco, CA: Berrett-Koehler.

32. Maheshwari, Varsha, 2010, "Corporate Social Responsibility: Creating Shared Value", Ajmer: *Economic Challenger*.

33. Margolis, J.D. and Walsh, J.P., 2001, People And Profits: *The Search For A Link Between A Company's Social And Financial Performance*, Mahwah, NJ: Lawrence Erlbaum Associates.

34. Mohan, A., 2001, "Corporate Citizenship: Perspectives From India", *Journal of Corporate Citizenship*.

35. Mullerat, Ramon. and Brennan, Daniel, 2005, *Corporate Social Responsibility: The Corporat Governance of The 21st Century*, The Netherlands: Kluwer Law International.

36. Ontiveros, Suzanne R., 1986, *Corporate Social Responsibility: Contemporary Viewpoints*, Abc-Clio.

37. Organisation for Economic Co-operation and Development, 2001, *Corporate Social Responsibility: Partners For Progress*, OECD Publishing.

38. Smith, A., 1976, *An inquiry into the nature and causes of the Wealth of Nations* Chicago: University of Chicago Press.

39. Visser, Wayne, et al., 2007, *The A To Z of Corporate Social Responsibility: A Complete Reference Guide to Concepts, Codes and Organisations*, John Wiley And Sons.

40. Vogel, David, 2005, *The Market For Virtue: The Potential and Limits of Corporate Social Responsibility*, Brookings Institution Press.

41. Welford, Richard, 2010, "Corporate Social Responsibility and Environmental Management", CSR Asia http://www3.interscience.wiley.com/journal/90513547/home. (accessed: 25/10/2010).

42. Werther, William B., and Chandler, David, 2006, *Strategic Corporate Social Responsibility: Stakeholders In A Global Environment*, Sage.

43. World Business Council For Sustainable Development, 1999, *Corporate Social Responsibility: Meeting Changing Expectations*, World Business Council For Sustainable Development.

44. Zerk, Jennifer A., 2006, *Multinationals and Corporate Social Responsibility: Limitations and Opportunities in International Law*, Cambridge University Press.

45. Asmus, P. (2003), "Corporate Social Responsibility [PDF document]", Retrieved from Lecture Notes Online Web site: http://www6.miami.edu/ethics/pdf_files/csr_guide.pdf

46. "Corporate Social Responsibility" (March 3, 2009), Retrieved August 9, 2009, from http://www.iocl.com/Aboutus/corporate social responsibility.aspx (accessed on 25/10/2010).

47. "Corporative social responsibility", Naukrihub, Retrieved on 9th August 2009, http://www.naukrihub.com/hr-today/corporate-social-responsibility.html, (accessed on 25/10/2010).

48. "Crisis management", Retrieved August 8, 2009, from wikipedia: http://en.wikipedia.org/wiki/Crisis_management, (accessed on 25/10/2010).

49. "CSR: A brand building exercise for media houses?" *Kalinga Time*, Retrieved from http://kalingatimes.com/business_news/news2/20090729_CSR_ A_brand_building_exercise_for_media_houses.html, (accessed on 25/10/2010).

50. Fauset, P., (2006), "What's wrong with Corporate Social Responsibility [PDF document]". Retrieved from Lecture Notes Online Web site: http://www.corporatewatch.org.uk/download.php?id=55 , accessed on 25/10/2010.

51. Shruti Das (2009), "Chicken soup", *Data Quest*, July 15, 2009, pp-12-14, 16-17.

Index

❑❑❑